mindful
games

PRAISE FOR *MINDFUL GAMES*

"The practical benefits of mindfulness are wide-ranging and undeniable. This wonderful book helps bring this transformative practice into the routines of those who will carry it into the future: our children."

—Congressman Tim Ryan

"*Mindful Games* is a remarkable book. It interweaves engaging and practical mindfulness exercises for children with a sophisticated and nuanced exploration of the psychology and insight wisdoms underlying them. This book is an invaluable resource for anyone with children in their lives—indeed, for anyone at all. Highly recommended."

—Joseph Goldstein, author of *Mindfulness: A Practical Guide to Awakening*

"In *Mindful Games*, Susan Kaiser Greenland offers a highly engaging and easy-to-understand set of activities to use with groups of children. All the games support understanding and empathy—and seem like fun! Susan draws on her own deep understanding of meditation and mindfulness practice, as well as her extensive knowledge of child development and research. Although written for adults working with groups of children, this book is certain to enrich the lives of any reader."

—Sharon Salzberg, author of *Lovingkindness* and *Real Happiness*

"Susan Kaiser Greenland captures the essence of mindfulness in a way that very few people can. As an experienced practitioner and teacher, her insight shines through on every page, and *Mindful Games* will undoubtedly be a wonderful resource for every parent and child alike."

—Andy Puddicombe, founder of Headspace

"We adults have a moral responsibility to do all we can to help young people develop the cognitive and emotional skills that will enable them not only to survive but to flourish in the world they have inherited from us. Susan Kaiser Greenland's latest book, *Mindful Games*, is a very welcome and important companion volume to her groundbreaking earlier book, *The Mindful Child*. I recommend it highly for its bountiful wisdom and skillful means, based on many years of her pioneering work in this field."

—B. Alan Wallace, author of *The Attention Revolution*

"Susan Kaiser Greenland, the pioneer in bringing mindfulness to young children, has done it again! *Mindful Games* is not only a fun way to teach and learn mindfulness but a truly wise way as well. Buy an extra copy because *Mindful Games* is destined to be one of the most beloved, well-worn references for parents, professionals, and kids alike."

—Christopher Willard, PsyD, author of *Growing Up Mindful*

"Illuminating ancient contemplative principles and applying them for serious and playful everyday use in practical exercises for youth and their families, this magnificent book offers us a powerful means for utilizing science-proven ways to strengthen a child or teen's mind by supporting the development of their brains and interpersonal relationships. You may even find, as I have, that these insightful ideas and games will enhance your own life as well. Soak in these words of wisdom, and enjoy the journey!"

—Daniel J. Siegel, MD, author of
Mind: A Journey to the Heart of Being Human

"A wonderful, fun, and engaging way to bring mindfulness into a child's life."

—Daniel Goleman, author of *Emotional Intelligence*

"Susan Kaiser Greenland has played a foundational role in making mindfulness practices developmentally appropriate for young people. In *Mindful Games*, she builds on her previous work by emphasizing *play* and *creativity* in teaching mindfulness skills. This is truly the way forward for making mindfulness a real exploration rather than just another chore or 'to do' for our kids."

—Chris McKenna, Program Director, Mindful Schools
(www.mindfulschools.org)

"In her marvelous new book, Susan Kaiser Greenland provides a whole new alphabet for raising better children as well as our best selves."

—Surya Das, author of *Awakening the Buddha Within*

"*Mindful Games* teaches mindfulness just as it should be taught—playfully. It's about the curiosity, exploration, and discovery that unfold with mindfulness, but mostly it's about the fun of it all!"

—Susan L. Smalley, PhD, Professor Emeritus, UCLA

mindful games

sharing mindfulness and meditation

with children, teens, and families

Susan Kaiser Greenland

Games edited by Annaka Harris

SHAMBHALA
BOULDER
2016

Shambhala Publications, Inc.
4720 Walnut Street
Boulder, Colorado 80301
www.shambhala.com

9 8 7 6 5 4 3

Printed in the United States of America

☉ This edition is printed on acid-free paper that meets the
American National Standards Institute Z39.48 Standard.
♻ Shambhala Publications makes every effort to print on recycled paper.
For more information please visit www.shambhala.com.

Distributed in the United States by Penguin Random House LLC
and in Canada by Random House of Canada Ltd

Designed by Allison Meierding

LIBRARY OF CONGRESS CATALOGING-IN-PUBLICATION DATA

Names: Greenland, Susan Kaiser, author. | Harris, Annaka, editor.
Title: Mindful games: sharing mindfulness and meditation
with children, teens, and families / Susan Kaiser Greenland;
games edited by Annaka Harris.
Description: First edition. | Boulder: Shambhala, [2016. |
Includes bibliographical references and index.
Identifiers: LCCN 2016007217 | ISBN 9781611803693 (pbk.: alk. paper)
Subjects: LCSH: Mindfulness (Psychology) |
Meditation. | Stress management.
Classification: LCC BF637.M4 G73 2016 | DDC 158.1—dc23
LC record available at https://lccn.loc.gov/2016007217

To Seth, Allegra, and Gabe

CONTENTS

INTRODUCTION

Meditation looks easy. How could sitting on a cushion and doing nothing be hard? Yet when I first learned to meditate, it reminded me of playing with a Russian nesting doll: open it and there's another just like it inside, only smaller, and then another, and several more, until the littlest doll is finally revealed. There seemed to be layers beneath layers of theory that I needed to understand before I could truly practice. Friends and colleagues had recommended several books, and I was having a hard time sorting through the different methods and terms; the progression of concepts and techniques seemed endless. But I stayed with it, and eventually meditation became a respite rather than a struggle. I finally had the littlest doll in hand. I wrote this book with the hope that it would make unpacking these ideas easier for other parents than it was for me and simple enough to share with their children.

A growing body of scientific research supports what contemplatives have known for centuries: mindfulness and meditation develop a set of *life skills* that allow children, teens, and parents to relate to what's happening within and around them with more wisdom and compassion. *Mindful Games* teaches six of these life skills—**Focusing**, **Quieting**, **Seeing**, **Reframing**, **Caring**, and **Connecting**. I present them in a circle with **Focusing** at the center because steady, flexible attention supports the other five.

Here's how they work together:

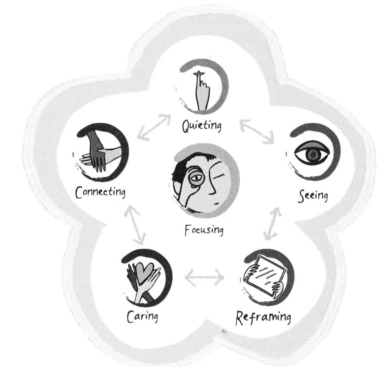

When children and teenagers **focus** on an experience in the present moment (the feeling of breathing, perhaps, or the sounds in a room), their minds tend to **quiet**, and a space opens up in their heads that allows them to see what's going on more clearly. As they become aware of what's happening in their minds and bodies, kids learn to use sense impressions ("I'm feeling restless," for instance, or "I have butterflies in my stomach") as cues to stop and reflect before speaking or acting. Through this process they become less reactive and more conscious of what's going on within and around them. Rather than focusing on the result, they **focus** on responding to the situation with wisdom and compassion. The qualities **caring** and **connecting** emerge naturally as children and teens see the web of relationships, causes, and conditions that lead up to each moment. Then they have an opportunity to **reframe** how they view a situation and can choose to speak and act in a way that's aligned with those qualities. These six life skills are scaffolded so that transforming attention (**Quieting, Focusing**) leads to transforming emotion (**Seeing, Reframing**), which leads to transforming speech, actions, and relationships (**Caring, Connecting**), a progression that's drawn from classical meditation training.

Over thousands of years, contemplatives have compiled an extensive catalog that maps our inner and outer worlds. I narrowed the catalog down to two lists that I introduce to kids and their parents through games, stories, guided visualizations, and demonstrations. The circle of six life skills is the first of those lists. The second list is made up of universal *themes* that inform a wise and compassionate worldview. They are:

Acceptance	Discernment
An open mind	Empathy
Appreciation	Everything changes
Attention (the spotlight and	Interdependence
the floodlight)	Joy
Attunement	Kindness
Behavioral restraint	Motivation
Cause and effect	Patience
Clarity	Present moment
Compassion	Self-compassion
Contemplative restraint	Wise confidence

Inherent in mindfulness and meditation are qualities that are mysterious, and trying to crack the code by boiling these qualities down to a couple of lists might seem to be missing this point entirely. I'm emboldened by other mysterious creative codes, however, such as jazz, where musicians study a circle of fifths and practice scales to fuel artistic qualities inherent in improvisation that are beyond description. Like jazz musicians, meditators study a set of themes and practice a set of life skills to fuel qualities inherent in mindfulness and meditation that are hard to pin down. In both creative disciplines, practitioners know these mysterious qualities when they see them, not because they're able to put them into words, but because they can feel them. There's an old saying that wisdom and compassion are like two wings of a bird and we need both to fly. The *conceptual* themes and *practical* life skills learned through mindfulness and meditation develop wisdom and compassion. Working together, they offer a degree of psychological freedom that, ideally, will help kids and their families to soar through life's difficulties, just as a bird takes flight and soars through the sky.

Perhaps what I like best about mindful games is that they offer parents and children a unique opportunity for coteaching and colearning. It's no surprise that many parents report that activities designed for kids offer them a way into meditation that they hadn't been able to access before. Which brings me to this important point: as parents, our own mindfulness has a powerful effect on everyone in our lives, especially on our children. They notice when we're calm, composed, and joyful, and they learn from our examples. How we steer our course through the world directly affects how secure they feel and how they move through the world. That's why I encourage parents to develop their own mindfulness first, by reflecting on the themes in this book and playing the games on their own, before sharing them with children.

Mindful games are written for youth, but don't let that fact fool you. They can be just as much fun and life changing for parents and for anyone who has a meaningful relationship with a child or teenager. Teachers, therapists, grandparents, aunts, uncles, troop leaders, and camp counselors, these games are for you, too. Ready to give one a try? Just relax and feel your feet.

feeling my feet

We pay attention to the feeling of the bottoms of our feet against the ground in order to relax, concentrate, and become aware of what's happening in this moment.

LIFE SKILLS Focusing, Caring   TARGET AGES All Ages

LEADING THE GAME

1. Sit or stand with your back straight and your body relaxed. Breathe naturally and notice what's happening in your body and mind right now.
2. Keep your body relaxed. If you're standing, keep your knees soft.
3. Now move your attention to the bottoms of your feet and notice how they feel against the ground. Let the thoughts and emotions that bubble up in your mind come and go.
4. Are you feeling your feet now? If not, don't worry. It's natural for your mind to wander. Just move your attention back to the bottoms of your feet to begin again.

TIPS

1. Focusing on a sensation like they do in *Feeling My Feet* helps children calm themselves when they feel overly excited or upset.
2. Vary the physical sensation that you ask kids to notice. For instance, ask children to feel the cool doorknob against the palm of their hands when they open the door, the warm water and soap-suds when they wash their hands, or the soft wool against their ankles and feet when they pull on their socks.
3. Consistency is more important than the length of time that children play mindful games, especially at first.

Part One

Quieting

The story "Goldilocks and the Three Bears" brings back fond memories, but I only recently saw its relevance to the nervous system. A blond-haired girl named Goldilocks discovers a cabin while walking through the forest. No one is there, but she marches in anyway. Goldilocks looks around and sees that it's the home of three bears—Momma Bear, Papa Bear, and Baby Bear. She spots three bowls of porridge on the kitchen table. Goldilocks is hungry, so she takes a bite from Momma's bowl, but it's "too hot!" Then from Papa's bowl: "It's too cold!" And from Baby's bowl: "It's just right." She gulps down the porridge and heads for the living room, where she finds three chairs. Momma and Papa Bears' chairs are too big, but, like the porridge, Baby Bear's chair is just right. You probably know the rest of the story: the Three Bears come home and find their porridge eaten, a chair broken, and Goldilocks sleeping upstairs in Baby Bear's bed. The lesson of "Goldilocks and the Three Bears," at least the way I tell the story, is that Goldilocks is remarkably in touch with her *window of tolerance*—a phrase coined by Dr. Daniel J. Siegel in *The Developing Mind* that indicates the range of arousal within which kids feel comfortable, remain engaged in what they're doing, and can be flexible in the way they respond to new ideas and situations. Not too hot, not too cold, just right.

Goldilocks, her nervous system, and her window of tolerance offer parents a peek into family life and interpersonal dynamics. Even though their routines couldn't be more different from those of contemplatives, children and families are increasingly drawn to meditation to help them manage stress and complicated emotions that feel intolerable. Unlike a contemplative existence, however, the demands of modern workaday life lead to an ongoing mild arousal of everybody's nervous system. In his book *Buddha's Brain*, the psychologist Dr. Rick Hanson calls this "life on simmer." For many, a little intensity nudges them to think and act more effectively, and a mild arousal of their nervous system is *just right*, just as Baby Bear's porridge and chair are *just right* for Goldilocks. In children for whom slight levels of arousal are outside of their windows of tolerance, even mild intensity disrupts their normal functioning and is definitely *not right*. It isn't a matter of personal preference, but a reflection of how their nervous systems operate. Even kids who thrive on simmer can be moved into a more rigid and reactive fight-or-flight mode by emotional triggers, and, just like everybody else, their windows of tolerance narrow when they feel tired, hungry, sick, stressed, afraid, or upset.

It's here that sharing mindfulness and meditation with youth can get tricky unless parents keep their children's nervous systems in mind. When children and teens are outside of their windows of tolerance they are in a less flexible, more reactive mode, one in which it's difficult—if not impossible—to be open to new ideas. There are times that kids simply don't have the bandwidth to be able to reflect on the big-picture themes that make up their own worldviews, much less on an alternative. They need help tolerating levels of stress and strong feelings that seem intolerable, and they want that help fast. Mindfulness-based **Quieting** tools can provide surprisingly quick short-term relief from overwhelming emotions. Once kids develop the confidence that strong emotions don't need to overpower them, even when their emotions are scary, they can continue deepening their exploration of mindfulness and meditation.

— 1 —

BREATHING
ON PURPOSE

When children tell me they can't handle stress and strong feelings, I'm reminded of Christopher Robin's advice to his friend Winnie-the-Pooh: "You're braver than you believe, and stronger than you seem, and smarter than you think." Yet becoming overwhelmed by strong emotions is common both on and off the meditation cushion. Children and teens can turn the tide if they shift their attention away from thinking about what's upsetting them and toward experiencing how they feel in the moment. When they do, their nervous systems settle, and some space opens up in their heads, allowing them to see and understand what led to their discomfort in the first place.

Scientists are beginning to understand how the brain helps children and teens regulate emotion. Some regions of the brain are linked to feelings of fear, anxiety, and other challenging emotions, while other regions enable kids to notice how they automatically react to these feelings and, in some cases, to alter the course of their emotional responses. Sometimes their automatic reactions are natural and entirely appropriate. When they step off the sidewalk without noticing a bus coming down the street, for instance, fear mobilizes their stress response so that they get out of the way in a hurry. Sometimes kids' stress responses are neither appropriate nor helpful, however. When they're behind in their schoolwork, for instance, the worry and fear that bubble up can motivate them to get the job done. But if kids get stuck on thinking about what will happen if they don't complete their assigned tasks on time, fear and worry can trigger more thoughts, which can trigger even stronger emotions, and on and on it goes. Then their thoughts and feelings are running the show. They know the seemingly endless loop of thinking that's running in their heads isn't helping them, yet they feel powerless to change anything. This is called *emotional hijack*—a term coined by the psychologist Dr. Daniel Goleman in his book *Emotional Intelligence*. Emotional hijack explains why it's tough for kids to think clearly when they feel overly excited or upset. Steady, flexible attention allows children and teens to avoid emotional hijack by recognizing when their thoughts and emotions begin to take over. Because children and teenagers' cognitive control is not yet fully developed, they are usually more susceptible to emotional hijack than their parents.

Kids' bodies manage stress through a variety of built-in mechanisms, ranging from chemical circuit breakers that shut off stress hormones to the complex, interrelated network of neural pathways known as the nervous system. When one of these mechanisms fires, all of the other mechanisms are affected. Mindful games that target stress management, pain management, and **Quieting** often encourage a light **Focus** on the out-breath because that simple shift in attention can ease physical and mental discomfort.

The nervous system—a complex network of cells with billions of connections that carry messages to and from the brain and spinal cord to and from all parts of the body—is divided into two inter-related branches known as the somatic and autonomic systems. The somatic system is involved in voluntary movements (jumping, walking, speaking); reflexive movements; and the sensations kids are aware of, such as pain and light. The autonomic system manages functions that happen largely outside of awareness, such as heart rate, blood pressure, and digestion. To better understand how emotional hijack and **Quieting** strategies work, let's take a closer look at how the nervous system functions in a crisis versus how it functions when kids are calm.

In an emergency, a branch of the autonomic nervous system called the sympathetic nervous system prepares kids' bodies to fight, flee, or freeze. In nonemergencies, a second branch called the parasympathetic nervous system allows their bodies to rest and digest. These two branches work together to keep children and teenagers balanced. Emotional hijack kicks the autonomic system into gear. Mindfulness-based **Quieting** tools also affect the autonomic system, but rather than intensifying the fight-or-flight response, these strategies tend to be calming.

The body's response to stress is complex, but as a general rule the baseline, balanced state of the autonomic nervous system is mostly resting and digesting, with a mild activation of the fight-or-flight response for alertness and vitality. This may surprise the many parents for whom a stressful life, and the adrenaline rush of a fight-or-flight response that comes with it, is their norm. Autonomic system functions are almost entirely independent of the conscious mind, but one aspect that children and teens have some control over is their breathing. When kids exhale, their brains send a signal down the vagus nerve—a long, complex cranial nerve that runs from the brain through the head, continues through the midsection, and ends in the belly—to slow their heartbeats. When kids inhale, that signal gets weaker, and their heartbeats quicken. Scientists have

referred to the vagus nerve as the single most important nerve in the body because of its role in supporting emotional-regulation, self-soothing, and social-engagement functions.

Long before scientists understood the connection, meditators and yogis used their breathing to tap into their autonomic nervous systems by lightly **Focusing** their attention on the in-breath for energy and alertness (arousing fight or flight) or on the out-breath for relaxation and calm (stimulating rest and digest). Young children in mindfulness classes have noticed this connection, too. After a brief mindful breathing game taught by Annaka Harris (one of the first to teach mindfulness and meditation in schools), an eight-year-old student at Toluca Lake Elementary School, in Toluca Lake, California, said, "I noticed that when I breathe in, my heart beats fast, and when I breathe out, my heart beats slowly."

Many children find the next game, which emphasizes the out-breath, to be calming.

breathing on purpose: a cooling out-breath

We learn that focusing on a long out-breath can be relaxing and help us feel calm.

LIFE SKILLS Focusing, Quieting   TARGET AGES All Ages

LEADING THE GAME

1. Sit with your back straight and your body relaxed and gently rest your hands on your knees. Breathe naturally while I count the length of your inhale and exhale.
   Count out loud, adjusting your pace to the natural rhythm of the child's breathing.

2. Now, breathe in for two counts and breathe out for four counts. *As the child increases the length of his exhale to four counts, adjust the pace of your counting so that it syncs with the pace of his breathing. (There is a natural pause between the inhale and exhale.) Continue for a few breaths.*

3. Let's go back to breathing naturally.

TIPS

1. Vary this game to help children feel alert and more awake by asking them to focus on a long in-breath. Follow the instructions for *A Cooling Out-Breath* but lengthen the inhale rather than the exhale (children will breathe in for four counts and out for two counts).

2. Introduce kids to *Breathing on Purpose* when they have some down-time, for instance, at the dinner table or in the carpool line. Once they understand that extending their exhale can cool them down, children can use their out-breath to **Quiet** their minds and bodies. Similarly, they can use a long inhale to help them feel more alert.

3. *Breathing on Purpose* is best practiced with an individual child rather than in a group.

When children or teens feel anxious or upset, encourage them to "breathe in a little bit and breathe out a whole lot," making a soft whooshing sound as they exhale. If a child is sobbing and having trouble catching his breath, ask him to raise his first finger and pretend it's a candle. Encourage him to breathe in through his nose to "smell the flowers," then to "blow out the candle" by pursing his lips and breathing out. Have kids blow so slowly and gently that the imaginary flame flickers instead of going out entirely. It can take a few breaths or a few minutes for his breathing to return to normal.

It doesn't matter whether children are sitting, standing, or lying down when they practice mindfulness and meditation. What's important is that in every posture they keep their spines relatively straight and their muscles relatively relaxed. The next game leads young children through a movement sequence that ends with them sitting or standing up straight. *Zip-Up*, along with several other movement activities in this book, is inspired by the work of the dance movement therapist Dr. Suzi Tortora, a friend, collaborator, and the author of *The Dancing Dialogue*. Rather than asking older children and teens to zip up, I ask them to sit or stand with their backs straight and their muscles relaxed.

zip-up

We imagine there's a zipper going up our bodies to help us keep our backs straight and muscles relaxed.

LIFE SKILLS Focusing   TARGET AGES Young Children

LEADING THE GAME

1. Let's pretend we have a zipper running up and down our bodies, from our belly buttons to our chins, that helps us sit or stand straight and tall.
2. Without touching your body, put one hand in front of your belly button and the other hand at your lower back, like this.
   Demonstrate by placing one hand in front of your belly button and the other hand at your lower back.
3. OK, let's zip ourselves up: *ZIIIPPP.*
   Demonstrate by moving your hands up your spine and chest, past your chin and head, ending with your hands in the air.
4. Now that we're zipped up, let's take a few breaths together with our bodies straight and tall.

1. Extend the game by adding a silent cheer at the end, while children still have their hands in the air.

2. Extend the game further with a mime that's similar to the song "Head, Shoulders, Knees, and Toes." Ask children to keep their eyes on you and follow your movements. No talking—only watching, listening, and mimicking. Sitting or standing tall, without saying a word, and while children follow your lead, touch your head with both hands, then your nose, your shoulders, your belly, and, if you like, your knees and toes. To make the game more challenging, you can mix up the sequence and speed up the pace. Alternating between big, small, fast, and slow movements gives children an opportunity to practice concentration and self-control.

Once kids are sitting or standing with their backs straight and their muscles relaxed, they're ready to play mindful games. Here's one that helps young children notice how different ways of breathing can change the way their minds and bodies feel. To play you'll need a pinwheel for each child and one for yourself.

breathing with a pinwheel

We blow on a pinwheel to notice that different ways of breathing—quick, slow, deep, and shallow—affect how our minds and bodies feel.

LIFE SKILLS Focusing, Seeing   TARGET AGES Young Children

LEADING THE GAME

1. Sit with your back straight and your body relaxed. Pick up your pinwheel.

2. We'll blow on our pinwheels together using long, deep breaths and notice how we feel.
   Talking points: Does your body feel calm and relaxed? Is it easy or hard for you to sit still after breathing deeply?
3. Now let's blow on our pinwheels using short, quick breaths.
   Talking points: How does your body feel now? Do you feel the same way after breathing quickly as you feel after breathing slowly?
4. Let's blow on our pinwheels now, breathing normally.
   Talking points: Was it easy to keep your mind on breathing, or were you distracted?

TIPS

1. Have a longer discussion about the different types of breathing: *Can you think of a situation when breathing deeply would be useful in daily life?* (Maybe to calm down when you're upset, or to help you concentrate.) *What about breathing quickly?* (Maybe when you're tired and want to feel a little more energized.)
2. When leading more than one child, ask them to put their pinwheels down before each set of talking points.

In the next section children will learn **Quieting** strategies in which they shift their attention away from thinking about what's upsetting them and toward a present moment—a sensation (something they hear, see, taste, touch, or smell), a word (counting breaths), or a task. If you ever squeezed on a stress ball or rubbed a worry stone, **Focusing** on sensations rather than thoughts is a familiar strategy. Many kids find these **Quieting** tools to be calming, which may be an indication that they decrease the fight-or-flight response in the nervous system and increase the rest-and-digest response.

2

ANCHORS FOR
ATTENTION

Kids are often encouraged to think through their problems in order to solve them. When they feel stressed and anxious, however, worrying about what's going on and endlessly mulling it over will heighten the body's stress response. The secret to putting the brakes on an overly heightened stress response lies in children's learning to notice when their bodies are sending them signals that anxious thoughts and feelings have started to take over. Then kids can relax and lightly **Focus** on a simple neutral object to anchor their attention. Perhaps because it is always with them, the most commonly used anchor is the sensation of breathing. It can be especially calming and self-soothing when kids place a hand on their hearts to feel their chests move up and down as they breathe. This suggestion comes from the Mindful Self-Compassion program developed by the psychologists and researchers Drs. Christopher K. Germer and Kristin Neff. Germer explains why anchors for attention are important, especially to manage strong emotions, in his book *The Mindful Path to Self-Compassion*: "Most of our mental suffering arises when our minds jump around from one subject to another, which is exhausting, or when we're preoccupied with unhappy thoughts and feelings. When we notice that the mind is behaving in this way, we need to give it an anchor—a place to go that's neutral and unwavering."

It's common to associate meditation with sitting still, but staying still can be hard for children and teens, especially when they feel stressed, anxious, or their minds are busy. That's one reason why mindful games in which kids walk, stretch, and shake are remarkably useful. Besides being fun, they offer children an opportunity to notice the differences in how their minds and bodies feel before and after they move. In *Trauma-Proofing Your Kids*, Dr. Peter Levine explains that structured physical activities are effective ways to release excess energy, especially when they're designed "so that highly energized periods of excitation are interspersed with equal periods of rest to give kids sufficient time for settling down. During both phases (the excitement and the settling), excess energy is automatically discharged." Periods of both excitement and settling are baked into the next game, which might be why kids report that *Shake It Up* calms them down when they're feeling overly excited or upset.

Sensations exist on a spectrum, with the strongest on one end and the weakest on the other. The strongest sensations are called "coarse" and the subtlest sensations are, not surprisingly, called "subtle." Coarse sensations are easier to focus on than subtle ones, and the fast movements in *Shake It Up* are an example of coarse sensory anchors. Focusing on a coarse sensation is a smart **Quieting** strategy because coarse sensory anchors grab kids' attention away from highly energized thoughts and feelings more easily than subtle sensations do. In a later section on **Focusing**, children will further refine and develop their attention skills by closely noticing subtle sensations when their minds and bodies are quiet.

shake it up

We shake our bodies to the sound of a drumbeat to release energy and help us focus.

LIFE SKILLS Focusing, Quieting   TARGET AGES All Ages

LEADING THE GAME

1. Let's pretend to put magic glue on the bottoms of our feet and glue them to the floor.
   Mime putting glue on the bottom of one foot and stomping it on the ground; then continue with the other foot. Children will follow your lead.

2. Can you wiggle your knees and keep the bottoms of your feet flat on the floor at the same time?
   Wiggle your knees while keeping the bottoms of your feet flat on the floor as if they're stuck.

3. Let's move our bodies to the sound of the drum, keeping our feet glued to the floor. Make big movements when you hear loud drumming.
   Drum loudly. Demo the movements as best you can while drumming.

4. Make small movements when you hear quiet drumming.
   Drum quietly. Demo the movements as best you can while drumming.

5. What do you do if you hear fast drumming?
   Drum quickly, and children will answer, "Move fast."

6. And if you hear slow drumming?
   Drum slowly, and children will respond, "Move slowly."

7. That's it. See if you can follow these sounds, and when the drumming stops, freeze.
   Alternate between fast, slow, loud, and quiet drumming. Children will freeze when the drumming stops.

8. Let's relax and feel our breathing for a few moments, and then we'll play again.

Run through the sequence again after children have had time to settle.

TIPS

1. If you don't have a drum you can slap your thighs to make a drumming sound.
2. Use shaking to break up a long period of sitting still.
3. Let children take turns leading too.
4. *Shake It Up* can be played sitting (at desks or in a circle on the floor) or standing.
5. There are times when shaking isn't a realistic option. In these situations, slowly swaying from side to side or squeezing a pillow are useful sensory anchors to help children settle.
6. Other sensory experiences that children and parents commonly use to calm and self-soothe are rocking back and forth, holding hands, hugging, and singing.

Interspersing gentle movement with periods of rest to discharge excess energy helps everyone **Quiet** their nervous system, not just kids. Tsokyni Rinpoche, the author of *Open Heart, Open Mind* and a Tibetan teacher with remarkable insight into Western psyches, draws upon this basic understanding when he teaches meditation to adults. (If you're not familiar with the word *Rinpoche*, it is an honorific title used in the Tibetan language to indicate that a teacher is an accomplished meditator.) Rinpoche's father, the late Tulku Urgyen Rinpoche, was born in Tibet and later settled in Nepal with his wife. He was one of the great meditation masters of modern times, and each of his four sons is now an important meditation teacher. I'm lucky to study with two of them—Tsokyni Rinpoche and his brother Yongey Mingyur Rinpoche who is also an author and the founder and guiding teacher of the Tergar meditation community.

The first time I took a class with Tsokyni Rinpoche, he started the week-long retreat with a movement-based practice designed to help us relax into our bodies and feelings. While sitting with our backs straight and our bodies relaxed, he asked us to raise our arms to shoulder height and shake them. On his signal, we were to breathe out forcefully and drop our arms and hands. We rested with our hands on our knees for a moment, without trying to control our thoughts and emotions. Rinpoche repeated the practice a few more times, asking us to shake our arms and hands again, drop them suddenly, and rest. In an article that was later published in *Lion's Roar*, he explained, "Whatever happens, wherever you land after dropping your arms, just let it be. Don't do or try to block anything. Just rest. There is no need to search for something new or try to achieve some special insight or state. Feel whatever feelings and sensations arise and be lightly aware of them. Feel them naturally and softly, and don't try to change anything. When uncomfortable feelings come up, you can relax and trust them, without analyzing or somehow figuring them out." Given what we know about the nervous system, it makes sense that Rinpoche's practice is calming. Woven through it are brief periods of excitement, brief periods of settling, and an emphasis on the out-breath—three strategies that likely work together to release excess energy and activate the rest-and-digest branch of the autonomic nervous system.

Rinpoche's instructions to rest with whatever feelings show up and let them be, without analyzing them or trying to figure them out, is another mindfulness-based strategy that can put the brakes on an overly heightened stress response. Young children are not yet developmentally ready to hold back from thinking about their thoughts and feelings, but older children and teens can give it a try, even though it sometimes feels counterintuitive.

Using a glitter ball (or, if one is not available, a snow globe or jar of water with baking soda in it) as a prop, the next demonstration helps children better understand how to dampen a heightened stress response. It employs a time-tested two-step strategy: having someone lightly **Focus** on a simple neutral object, to anchor their attention, and leave their thoughts and feelings alone. The glitter in the ball represents stress and strong emotions. When you shake the ball, the particles whirl about, making the water cloudy. When you leave the ball alone, the water slowly clears. This visual experiment—the equivalent of going from feeling calm and clear-eyed to feeling stressed and overwhelmed and then back to feeling settled—helps kids connect the activity in the ball to the activity in their minds and bodies.

seeing clearly

We shake a glitter ball to help us understand the connection between what happens in our minds and what happens in our bodies.

LIFE SKILLS Focusing, Seeing   TARGET AGES All Ages

LEADING THE GAME

1. *Talking points: Can you describe how your body feels when you're stressed? Can you describe what your mind is like when you're stressed? When you feel stressed, can you think clearly?*
2. When the ball is still, like it is now, can you see through the water to the other side?
3. What do you think will happen if I shake the ball? Will you be able to see through the water?
   Shake the ball. The glitter will whirl about, and the water will become cloudy.

4. Now place your hand on your belly and feel your breathing. *Stop shaking the ball, and the glitter will settle.*

5. Can you see through the water now?

6. Did the glitter go away? Nope, it's still there. Thoughts are like that, too. Our minds can get so busy that we can't think clearly. But if we feel our breathing and leave our thoughts alone, they settle down, and we can think clearly again.

7. Let's try it once more. *Repeat the demonstration.*

TIPS

1. It's helpful to generate a little energy up front with a brief period of physical activity so that the child is able to feel herself settle during the demonstration. If she feels focused, calm, and relaxed before the demonstration, she probably won't feel differently at the end.

2. Meditation isn't about having a blank mind or getting rid of thoughts, yet some children think it is. Kids can also believe that it's "bad" to have thoughts when they meditate. If you point out that thoughts and emotions are beautiful, just like the glitter that's swirling around in the ball, children can then see that even beautiful thoughts can be distracting.

3. Once a young child understands the metaphor, use a phrase like "See if you can settle your glitter" as a gentle prompt for him to focus on his breathing when he feels overly excited or upset.

4. Point out that meditation doesn't get rid of the stress in everyday life just like the glitter doesn't go away when it settles at the bottom of the ball. Even though meditation doesn't get rid of stress entirely, it can help us manage stress by teaching us to relax and let our minds settle when we feel overly excited or upset. Then we can see what's happening in and around us clearly.

Quieting tools are of no use if kids don't believe there's a connection between what they think and how they feel. The next game allows skeptics to experience a mind-body connection firsthand by imagining that they're biting into a lemon. Just thinking about biting a lemon usually makes kids' mouths pucker up or water, even when there's not a lemon in sight.

mind-body connection

We imagine biting into a lemon to help us understand the connection between what's happening in our minds and what's happening in our bodies.

LIFE SKILLS Focusing, Seeing   TARGET AGES Older Children, Teens

LEADING THE GAME

1. *Talking points: Can your thoughts change how your body feels? Can how your body feels change your thoughts? Can your emotions change how your body feels? Can how your body feels change your emotions?*

2. Resting your hands on your knees, sit with your back straight and your body relaxed and close your eyes.

3. Picture yourself sitting at a kitchen table. There's a lemon in front you. Imagine picking up the lemon. Imagine that it's wet and cold in your hand. Picture yourself cutting the lemon in half, picking up one half, smelling the lemon, and then biting into it. Is anything happening in your mouth?

4. *Talking points: Did your body react to thinking about biting into a lemon as if you were actually doing it? Is this an example of a mind-body connection? Can you give other examples of mind-body connections?*

The games *Mind-Body Connection* and *Seeing Clearly* lay the conceptual groundwork for conversations about heightened stress, psychological pressure, and how to mitigate their negative effects. When I ask children and teenagers for examples of how their minds have affected their bodies, it's common for them to report that their stomachs ache when they're anxious or that they have trouble sleeping when they're worried or overly excited. Because it can be reassuring for them to know that they're not alone in these experiences, I find it helpful to share similar ones that I've had. When offering examples of mind-body connections, don't forget to include thoughts and emotions that make you feel better, too. This will set the stage for similar discussions that you'll have in connection with the kindness visualizations that come later in this book.

Part Two

Seeing
&
Reframing

Two young fish are swimming along. They happen to meet an older fish swimming the other way who nods at them and says, "Morning, boys. How's the water?" The two young fish swim on for a bit, and then eventually one of them looks over at the other and asks, "What the heck is water?"

The point of this story, the one that David Foster Wallace told at the start of his 2005 commencement address to the graduates of Kenyon College, is that the most obvious and fundamental facts of life are often the hardest ones to see and talk about. I was reminded of Wallace's fish story when I was teaching in a research study at the University of California, Los Angeles (UCLA), early childcare centers, and saw the vocabulary word *atmosphere* written on the white board in a preschool classroom. I asked the executive director, Gay MacDonald, if the word *atmosphere* was over the heads of my four-year-old students. She reminded me that little children can learn big words if they're taught in an appropriate context. The big-picture concepts threaded through contemplative training can be explained plainly and taught playfully, even if they're well outside of children's developmental ranges. Just as the young fish in Wallace's story quite happily swim in something they can't name, children quite happily embody qualities of wisdom and compassion they can't yet conceptually understand. Many of us who have practiced meditation for quite a while are humbled to say that some of those qualities are beyond our conceptual understanding, too.

Meditation has a few things in common with gardening, and one of them is the importance of preparation. The biggest mistake beginning gardeners make is to plant seeds before preparing the soil. Just as it takes sustained physical effort to remove rocks from garden beds prior to planting, it takes sustained mental effort to uncover patterns of thought and behavior that cause suffering. It takes even more sustained effort to change them. Changing patterns and behaviors requires a shift in worldview, and, more often than not, that tends to be a long and bumpy process. There's no reason for kids to be discouraged, though. They need only remember that it's more helpful to approach this internal work with a gentle touch and sense of humor than with a mental equivalent of the pickax that gardeners use to remove rocks from the soil.

3

AN OPEN MIND

My grown son tells me that he still finds this story to be a helpful reminder that we never know for sure what will happen next.

A father and his son wake up one morning and learn that their horse has run away. Word travels fast, and when their neighbor hears the news, she exclaims, "What rotten luck!" The farmer replies, "We'll see."

The horse returns and brings with him a gorgeous stallion. Their neighbor calls out, "How wonderful!" and the farmer says, "We'll see."

The farmer's son mounts the stallion, but the horse starts bucking, and the farmer's son is thrown to the ground while trying to control him. He breaks his leg. The neighbor shouts, "How terrible!" Again the farmer replies, "We'll see."

War breaks out, and the other young men in the village are drafted into the army, but the farmer's son stays behind because he has a broken leg. The neighbor congratulates the farmer, who shrugs and says, "We'll see."

Through mindfulness and meditation, kids—and their parents—become comfortable with complexity and uncertainty, just like the farmer in this story. Many of us find this to be a relief. Joseph Goldstein, a pioneering American meditation teacher and cofounder of the Insight Meditation Society, once gave a talk in Los Angeles in which he spoke about trying to untangle inconsistencies between two schools of contemplative thought. Goldstein told the crowded auditorium that he struggled to figure out which view was correct until he realized that one didn't have to be right and the other wrong. "Well," he said, "that was a relief." Seven years after this talk, he elaborated on the relief of not knowing in an article posted on the PBS television network's website:

We don't know a lot. We don't know much more than we know. And it's a relief to let go of our attachment to views, our attachment to opinions, especially about things we don't know. A new mantra began to form in my mind: "Who knows?" This not knowing is not a quality of bewilderment; it's not a quality of confusion. It actually is like a breath of fresh air, an openness of mind. Not knowing is simply holding an open mind regarding these very interesting questions to which we might not yet have answers.

When older children, especially teenagers, become comfortable with not having all the answers, the negative connotation that's usually associated with not knowing can get turned on its head. Having relaxed their need to pin down an answer immediately, kids are able to respond to whatever's happening with less urgency. Then they can be more receptive to other points of view and curious about what might be waiting for them just around the corner. The same holds true for parents. Myla Kabat-Zinn and her husband, Dr. Jon Kabat-Zinn, speak about the benefits of keeping an open mind in their parenting book *Everyday Blessings*. Jon Kabat-Zinn is the standard-bearer for the secular mindfulness movement, having developed the Mindfulness-Based Stress Reduction (MBSR) program at the University of Massachusetts Medical School and having written many books about mindfulness. As he and his wife write:

> *Mindful parenting involves keeping in mind what is truly important as we go about the activities of daily living with our children. Much of the time, we may find we need to remind ourselves of what that is or even admit that* we may have no idea at the moment, *for the thread and meaning and direction in our lives is easily lost. But even in our most trying, sometimes horrible moments as parents, we can deliberately step back and begin afresh, asking ourselves as if for the first time and with fresh eyes, "What is truly important here?"*

Every experience is unique, and there are an infinite number of causes and conditions that lead up to each moment. Even when kids do their best to look at an experience from every angle, they can't possibly uncover them all. In *Beyond Religion*, the Dalai Lama, who is the spiritual leader of Tibet, points out that no matter how hard we try we can never see the entire picture. To get a sense of what he means, take a moment to reflect on the remarkable web of changing causes and conditions that led to this moment. If your parents had never met, you wouldn't have been born. If your grandparents hadn't met, your parents wouldn't have set foot on this earth, and you wouldn't be here either. Generation after generation of your ancestors met and had a child, who was one of countless links in a series of causal connections that made it possible for you to read this book. Unless you're my blood relative, I'm a cause and condition that sprung from an entirely different family tree. If each of my ancestors hadn't lived, loved, and had children, you couldn't read this book, because I wouldn't be here to write it. Regardless of whether we both got here as the result of a divine plan, a wild stroke of luck, or something in between, our planet, along with everything and everyone on it, is an always changing, interdependent, and mysterious puzzle. The Dalai Lama offers some reassurance regarding this potentially overwhelming concept:

> *Of course, no matter how hard we may try, human discernment is always incomplete. Unless we are clairvoyant or omniscient, like Buddha or like God, we will never see the entire picture, and we will never know all the causes that have given rise to any situation. Nor can we foresee all the consequences of our actions. There is always bound to be some element of uncertainty. It is important to acknowledge this, but it should not worry us. Still less should it make us despair of the value of rational assessment. Instead it should temper our actions with proper humility and caution. Sometimes, admitting that we do not know an answer can be helpful in itself.*

Even young children, who aren't yet ready to understand the crazy quilt of causes and conditions that lead up to every moment, can feel more secure in the face of uncertainty by becoming comfortable with the idea that they don't need to know the answer to every question. In *I Wonder*, Annaka Harris's picture book with illustrations by John Rowe, Eva and her mom walk through the woods on a moonlit night. When Eva's mom asks her a question, Eva seems perplexed about not knowing the answer. Eva's mom reassures her, "It's OK to say I don't know." After all, parents don't know the answer to every question, either. Buoyed by newfound confidence, Eva's creativity is unleashed, and she asks one question after another: "How do the moon and the earth stay close together?" "Are they friends?" "Where was the butterfly before she came to visit me?" Instead of feeling uncomfortable with uncertainty, Eva is now excited by the mysteries in life that she and her mom are able to explore together.

In the next game, young children guess what's inside a mysterious-looking box. *Mystery Box* is a playful springboard into discussions about what it's like to start something new, to not know the answer to a question, and to not know what will happen next. Prepare by filling the mystery box with playful objects outside of the children's sight and then placing the closed box a short distance away in front of the children.

mystery box

When we guess what's inside a mysterious box, we notice how it feels when we're asked a question and don't know the answer.

LIFE SKILLS Seeing, Reframing   TARGET AGES Young Children

LEADING THE GAME

1. Let's guess what's inside the mystery box.
   Listen to children's guesses.
2. *Talking points: What does it feel like to not know what's in the box? Do you feel excited? Frustrated? Something else?*
3. *Hold the box and feel it, look at it, and shake it—but don't open it.*
   Do you have any more guesses about what might be inside?
   Listen to children's guesses.
4. Let's open it and see.
5. *Talking points: How does it feel when you don't know what's going to happen next? Do you like trying new things, or would you rather not try something new? What is it like to expect one thing but find another? How do you feel when you have to wait for something (to open a present, to go to a friend's house, or for a turn on the swing)?*

1. Ideas for things to put in the box: paper clips, flowers, balloons, Legos, or erasers.
2. For very young children, it helps to give examples of things that might be in the box before they begin guessing.
3. Have children take turns putting something in the box while everyone else guesses.

The Big Picture reminds older children and teens that they can do their research, weigh everything they've learned before reaching a conclusion, and still not have enough information to answer a question correctly. It's helpful to show children a picture of several people with their eyes closed, touching different parts of an elephant, before leading the game.

the big picture

We imagine what it would be like to guess what something is by touching only one part of it with our eyes closed. We learn that what we believe depends on the information we have.

LIFE SKILLS Seeing, Reframing   TARGET AGES All Ages

LEADING THE DISCUSSION

1. What if you were asked to touch one part of an elephant with your eyes closed and guess what you were touching? Would you be able to guess correctly?
   - If you touched only the elephant's *trunk*, what would you think it was? (Hint: the elephant's trunk is long and round like a snake or a hose.)
   - If you touched just the elephant's *leg*, what would you think it was? (Hint: the elephant's leg is big and round like a tree trunk.)
   - If you touched only the elephant's *tusk*, what would you think it was? (Hint: the elephant's tusk is sharp like a knife.)
   - If you touched just the elephant's *ear*, what would you think it was? (Hint: the elephant's ear is thin and wide like a fan.)
2. *Talking points: Tell a story about a time that you misunderstood someone because you didn't have all the information. Tell a story about a time that someone misunderstood you because he or she didn't know the whole story.*

TIPS

1. Adapt *The Big Picture* for a younger child by placing a large stuffed animal out of sight a short distance away. Then have her guess what the animal is by closing her eyes and touching just one part of the stuffed animal (a leg, an ear, a round belly). If you think it will be hard for her to keep her eyes closed in the excitement, we use a blindfold (like in the game pin the tail on the donkey).

More often than not, children are unable to guess what they are touching because they can't see the big picture. What if children *are* able to see the big picture, though, but they see it differently? Does one child have to be right and the other one wrong? Or is it possible for some things to be more than one thing at the same time? Children find out in *Duck! Rabbit!*, a game based on a famous optical illusion that can be seen as either a duck or a rabbit, but not as both simultaneously. This ambiguous drawing was first popularized by the American psychologist Joseph Jastrow in the early twentieth century. It is well known in philosophical circles through the work of the Austrian-British philosopher Ludwig Wittgenstein. For the next game, use the duck/rabbit drawing that is printed in the appendix.

duck! rabbit!

We pay close attention to a drawing that looks like both a duck and a rabbit, to better understand how some things can be more than just one thing.

LIFE SKILLS Seeing, Reframing TARGET AGES All Ages

LEADING THE DISCUSSION

1. Let's look at the drawing together.
   Show everyone the illustration.
2. Is it a duck or a rabbit?
   Wait for children to answer, and then offer your guess too. (If either the duck or rabbit wasn't selected by any of the players, choose that one and explain to children how it can be seen as that animal too.)

3. Look again, and see if it looks different to you now. What do you think? Is it a duck or a rabbit?
4. Who's right and who's wrong?
5. Let's look at the drawing one more time. What does it look like now? Did you change your mind?
6. *Talking points: Do you think the drawing is really supposed to be a duck or a rabbit? Could it be both?*

TIPS

1. Amy Krouse Rosenthal and Tom Lichtenheld have created an ingenious picture book based on the duck/rabbit drawing that you can read with your child to extend your conversation about these talking points.

Using hand gestures to respond to questions, the next game also demonstrates that complexity and contradiction exist everywhere, even in common daily events.

pinky pointing

We point a pinky finger—up, down, and to the side—to help us notice how we're feeling and communicate it to others.

LIFE SKILLS Seeing, Reframing   TARGET AGES All Ages

LEADING THE GAME

1. We can feel a lot of different ways—sometimes we feel happy, sometimes sad, sometimes tired, sometimes excited—and these are all natural feelings. There's no right or wrong way to feel, and our feelings change. We probably feel different now than we did this morning, and we'll feel different later in the day than we do now.

Sometimes we feel the same as one another, sometimes we feel different, and either way is OK.

2. Take a breath and notice how you're feeling right now.

3. I'm going to ask a question, and everyone will share their answers at the same time by pointing a pinky finger when I say, "1-2-3-GO."

4. The question is: "Is it easy to sit still, or is it hard to sit still right now?" If it's easy, point your pinky to the ground; if it's hard, point your pinky to the sky; and if it's in between, point your pinky to the side. 1-2-3-GO.

5. Keep your pinky pointing, so we can all see how everyone is feeling right now. Remember, there's no right or wrong way to answer. Interesting!

Continue asking questions as long as children remain engaged.

TIPS

1. *Pinky Pointing* is a fun and efficient way to ask logistical questions ("Who'd like to take a break?"), but generally we use it to investigate how children feel in that moment. For instance, you might ask, "Do you have a lot of energy, or do you feel tired? Do you feel calm or excited? Do you feel relaxed or tense?"

2. By keeping their pinkies in the air and looking around, children see how others answered the same question. Differences of opinion are to be expected, and it is eye opening for some children to learn that not everyone shares their opinion. On the other hand, children who feel like they're isolated from the larger group are often pleased to see that others answer a question the same way that they answer it.

3. To reduce a positive or negative association with a specific hand gesture, change what the pinky up, down, or sideways represents. For example, if pinky up means "hard to sit still" in the first round, switch directions so that pinky up means "easy to sit still" in the next round. This undermines the reflexive judgments that are often associated with an answer (anger is bad, gratitude is good) and creates an environment in which children can observe what's

Minds are a bundle of multifaceted, and sometimes contradictory, thoughts, feelings, and beliefs. Yet, in an effort to make sense of and control what's happening within and around them, kids can oversimplify their experiences. Kids (and parents) have a tendency to reduce aspects of their internal worlds into categories by labeling them black or white, good or bad, right or wrong, duck or rabbit. They have a tendency to compartmentalize what happens in their external worlds, too. But life is far too complex for this type of binary thinking, and life experiences generally don't fall into such neat categories. The life skills **Seeing** and **Reframing** develop children and teenager's capacities to hold back from jumping to conclusions and reflexively making judgments. Instead, they learn to view an experience with an open mind, in all its wonder and complexity. F. Scott Fitzgerald describes an open mind in his well-known quote, "The test of a first-rate intelligence is the ability to hold two opposed ideas in mind and still retain the ability to function." Mindfulness and meditation help kids learn to do just that. Young meditators discover that even opposites are interdependent, and both can be held in mind at the same time—for instance, yin and yang, buyer and seller, teacher and student, or parent and child.

— 4 —

APPRECIATION

Holding on to anything too tightly is stressful. This insight can be traced back to the historical Buddha, a prince named Siddhartha Gautama, who was born in northern India sometime between four and six hundred years before the Common Era. To his father's chagrin, when the prince was twenty-nine years old he gave up a cushy royal life to become a wandering monk. After several years of wandering, the Buddha sat down to meditate under a bodhi tree in Bodh Gaya, India, and vowed to stay until he became enlightened. There he had four insights into human existence: suffering is part of life (not all of life, just part of life); there's a cause for suffering; there's an end to suffering; and—here's the best part—there's a means by which we can end suffering. Over the next twenty-five hundred years or so, scientists, philosophers, and poets have affirmed these four insights across disciplines. In one of his best-known books, *Oh, the Places You'll Go!*, Dr. Seuss restates the first insight in rhyme: "I'm sorry to say so / but, sadly, it's true / that Bang-ups and Hang-ups / *can* happen to you." The next story is one of my favorites to illustrate how holding on to something too tightly can cause unnecessary pain.

A hunter sets a monkey trap by putting a banana inside a bamboo cage. The bars on the cage are placed just widely enough apart for a monkey to reach inside with a flat hand, but not widely enough to pull his hand out if he's holding a banana. The monkey happens upon the trap, sees the banana, reaches in, and grabs it. Once he gets hold of the banana, he won't let it go, and he's caught. Freedom is as close as releasing his grip, but the monkey is sure that he needs this very banana and won't let it go.

The monkey is caught in a familiar trap. He's chasing what he thinks will make him happy (eating the banana) and avoiding what he thinks will make him unhappy (losing the banana). Is the moral of this story to drop the banana? Sometimes, but not always. If we're actually caught in a trap, dropping the metaphorical banana is definitely the way to go. The cause-and-effect relationship between our metaphorical bananas and our suffering is usually more nuanced than in this story, however. Often, the more skillful response to suffering is to let it alone rather than these two more common responses—to ignore the pain entirely or to consider it from every angle. Here's the problem with these two responses: When we ignore our suffering, or chew it over time and time again, our discomfort is likely to escalate. We can exit this familiar pattern by relating to suffering differently and choosing to experience it rather than sweeping it under the rug or analyzing it. Then, the activity in our minds can settle, allowing us to see what's happening within and around us more clearly and with less reactivity. Because this way of relating to physical and emotional pain is a shift away from the norm that takes some time to figure out and longer to execute, there's plenty of suffering along the way, even for the most experienced meditators.

Fortunately, suffering can yield important insights. The essayist and novelist Pico Iyer considered the value of suffering on the opinion page of the *New York Times*:

Wise men in every tradition tell us that suffering brings clarity, illumination; for the Buddha, suffering is the first rule of life, and insofar as some of it arises from our own wrongheadedness— our cherishing of self—we have the cure for it within. Thus in certain cases, suffering may be an effect, as well as a cause, of taking ourselves too seriously. I once met a Zen-trained painter in Japan, in his 90s, who told me that suffering is a privilege, it moves us toward thinking about essential things and shakes us out of shortsighted complacency; when he was a boy, he said, it was believed you should pay for suffering, it proves such a hidden blessing.

Suffering becomes a hidden blessing when older kids (and parents) are able to take advantage of the opportunity suffering offers to become more aware of what's happening within and around them. When we notice that health and well-being are fragile and transient, we see the theme everything changes manifested in daily life. When we recognize that our own happiness is complex, changing, and coexistent with the happiness of others, we acknowledge another theme, our interdependence. When we remember that thoughts and feelings are also complex, interrelated, and in flux, we practice a third theme, keeping an open mind, while giving the previous two themes a nod. And when we accept that bad things happen to good people, we recognize the first insight of mindfulness—that suffering is part of life. Reflections like these, the ones that tend to come in the wake of suffering, lead to increased clarity about whatever is happening and make it tough to take petty concerns too seriously. Pico Iyer points to self-cherishing as a cause and effect of suffering, and it's natural to be preoccupied by self-centered concerns when life is good. When life is challenging, however, reflections on the themes of interdependence, everything changes, clarity, acceptance, and an open mind encourage us to step back and see the vast field of causes and conditions that make up the larger picture of our suffering (in other words, to recognize the theme of cause and effect). As our lenses enlarge, self-centered concerns are often dwarfed by more fundamental issues and seem unimportant in comparison. An appreciation of the flip side of suffering can emerge when we recognize the people, places, and things that help make suffering bearable. Then, even though we're in pain, it's relatively easy to hold other people in mind with appreciation and kindness, two more themes that are woven through a wise and compassionate worldview.

Kids don't need to suffer in order to broaden their mind-sets, though. The next game uses a simple approach that can be summed up by this Vietnamese proverb: "When eating a fruit, think of the person who planted the tree." *Thank the Farmer* heightens young children's awareness of the theme interdependence while giving them an opportunity to practice two other themes that children are reflecting on in this section, kindness and appreciation. Older children and teens might be too old for *Thank the Farmer*, but they can benefit from reflecting on the Vietnamese proverb upon which it is based. Prepare by finding a comfortable place where the children can eat and placing a few raisins in a cup for each child.

thank the farmer

Before eating a raisin, we thank the people, places, and things that were part of its journey from grapevine to table.

LIFE SKILLS Seeing, Reframing   TARGET AGES Young Children

LEADING THE GAME

1. Let's pick up a raisin. But before we eat it, we'll think about how it got from the grapevine into our hands:
   - Think of the worms that nourished the soil . . . *Thank you, worms!*
   - Think of the sun and rain that fed the vines . . . *Thank you, nature!*
   - Think of the farmers who took care of the vines and harvested the grapes . . . *Thank you, farmers!*
   - Think of the workers who harvested the grapes, put them out to dry, and boxed them up as raisins . . . *Thank you, workers!*
   - Think of the truck drivers who drove the raisins to the store . . . *Thank you, truck drivers!*
   - Think of the person who bought the raisins and brought them to you . . . (Children thank you.)
2. You're welcome! Now, let's eat the raisin. Put it in your mouth for a moment, without chewing, and notice what that feels like. Then spend a moment chewing. And, finally, swallow. Pay careful attention to how each step feels.
3. *Talking points: Have you thought about your food this way before? Do you think about raisins differently now?*

There's a common tendency to pay more attention to what we *don't have* than to be grateful for what we *do have*. At times parents want more—a better job, a longer vacation, or more money in the bank—and at times we want less—a lower credit card bill or a smaller number when we stand on the scale. And at times we want more for our children and families than we're able to provide. In all of these examples, we're focused on what we lack rather than on what we have. Some scientists chalk this negative bias up to evolution. They suggest that brains are hardwired to respond more strongly to bad news than to good news because, from a brain's perspective, bad news signals danger, and our brains evolved to prioritize survival over everything else. But we can turn this negative bias around by reflecting on and appreciating what we have in our lives already.

To prepare for the next game, cut strips of construction paper and place them in a basket, along with decorating materials.

appreciation chain

We write notes of appreciation to remind ourselves of what we have and to see the positive effect of a simple act of kindness.

LIFE SKILLS Seeing, Reframing   TARGET AGES Young Children

LEADING THE GAME

1. *Talking points: What are some ways people have helped you? What is "appreciation" or "gratitude"?*
2. Let's make an appreciation chain together. First we'll write down things we're grateful for on these strips of paper. Then we'll decorate them and connect them into a chain.
3. *Talking points: How do you feel when you appreciate something or someone? What are some of the ways that we're all connected? What is a community?*
   When the chain is ready, help children hang it in a meaningful place or give it away as a gift.

1. Appreciation games reinforce the theme of interdependence by reminding kids that they're connected to people they know and to people they don't know in ways that are hard to imagine. For instance, many, many people participate in bringing their meals to the table (farmers, grocers, cooks) and in making their favorite television show or movie (writers, executives, actors, directors).

Painful thoughts and emotions sometimes show up when children and teens practice appreciation and kids can easily misinterpret parents' reminders to be thankful as an indication that we're minimizing their challenges, even when that's not the case. When painful emotions do come up, encourage kids to view how they feel through a wide lens, not to gloss over their feelings or push them aside. When kids acknowledge their hurt feelings and remember the good things in their lives, they embody one of the themes they've been exploring—an open mind. *Three Good Things* gives children a chance to practice this holistic mind-set when they're upset and they need it the most.

three good things

When faced with a disappointment, we acknowledge our feelings, and then we think of three good things in our lives, too.

LIFE SKILLS Seeing, Reframing   TARGET AGES All Ages

LEADING THE DISCUSSION
1. Do you ever feel disappointed by something or someone?
   Listen to children's stories.

2. How did that make you feel?
Acknowledge children's feelings and, if appropriate, talk about them.
3. I bet even when you're feeling disappointed there are good things happening in your life, too. Let's name three good things together.

TIPS

1. Remind children that the point of this game isn't to pretend they're not upset when they feel upset. It's to remember that they can feel two things at once: they can feel grateful for good things while feeling sad, hurt, or disappointed by challenges.
2. If children or teens have trouble thinking of three good things on their own, brainstorm and help them discover some.
3. When kids understand that this game is not about sweeping their feelings under the rug, the phrase "three good things" can become a playful and humorous response to the minor gripes that show up in family life. For instance, if a young child spills a glass of apple juice and looks like he's going to cry, you can respond with something like, "Ahhh, that can be frustrating. Can you name *Three Good Things* while I wipe the counter?"
4. Parents can encourage kids to remind them to name *Three Good Things* when they're stuck on a trivial disappointment or minor annoyance, too.
5. To develop a habit of thankfulness, play *Three Good Things* around the dinner table, before bedtime, and at other times when the family is together (and no one is upset).

The next game, *Life Is Good*, is a playful way for kids to practice acknowledging their challenges, and then placing them into a broader context by naming a few positive things that are in their lives, too—I jokingly call it *The Whining Game*. Kids roll a ball back and forth in a circle or between partners. Whoever has the ball names something that gets on her nerves. Then she rolls the ball to another player while saying, ". . . and life is good." This game was inspired by a gratitude practice that James Baraz, a founding teacher of Spirit Rock Meditation Center, taught to his eighty-nine-year-old mother, and the title of this game was a welcome suggestion from the pioneering meditation teacher Joseph Goldstein.

life is good

As we roll a ball back and forth (or around in a circle), we name things that bother us, while remembering the good things in life by adding, ". . . and life is good."

LIFE SKILLS Seeing, Reframing   TARGET AGES All Ages

LEADING THE GAME
1. We're going to roll this ball to one another, and when the ball comes to you, name one thing that's bothering you. Then roll the ball to the next person and say, ". . . and life is good."
2. I'll go first. *I lost my necklace today . . .*
   Roll the ball to another player while saying, ". . . and life is good."
3. Now you name something and roll the ball.
   Guide players in speeding up the pace as the play continues.

At first, thankfulness may feel like a mere intellectual exercise. Yet the more families carve out time to practice appreciation when life is good, the easier it is for parents and children to be thankful for the good things in life when times are hard. When that shift happens, appreciation becomes an integral part of a family's worldview and is no longer just an intellectual exercise.

— 5 —

WHAT'S
HAPPENING NOW

Since I attended my first meditation retreat, mindfulness and meditation have gone from the social fringes to the cover of *TIME Magazine*. Still, to borrow from Dan Harris, author of *10% Happier*, whose job as a network news anchor is about as mainstream as you can get, mindfulness and meditation have a "woo-woo" problem. Blogs and other popular writing hype, overpromote, and oversimplify these two words to create vague and inaccurate new meanings. They are often used interchangeably, and to add to the confusion, somewhat random concepts are conflated and called "mindfulness" or "meditation." I wish I could shrug off these definitional differences, but they matter.

The word *meditation* is defined in different ways among contemplative traditions. In his book *Happiness*, Dr. Matthieu Ricard, a French author and Tibetan monk, explains that the term for meditation in Tibetan means "familiarization," as in "familiarizing yourself with a new vision of things, a new way to manage your thoughts, of perceiving people and experiencing the world." Similarly, I use the word *meditation* to describe a method through which we familiarize ourselves with our minds by working with them directly to develop steady, flexible attention; investigate what's happening within and around us; increase our insight into other people, the world, and ourselves; and strengthen positive qualities, like the themes we're exploring in this book.

The word *mindfulness* comes from the ancient languages Sanskrit and Pali, in which it is defined as "remembering"—as in remembering the object of our attention. Keeping our minds on a chosen object and not getting lost in distraction are the functions of mindful attention. In classical writing, the word *mindfulness* is often used together with the words *awareness* or *knowing*. In this context, the words *knowing* and *awareness* refer to our capacity to notice what is going on in our minds. With mindfulness, we have a heightened awareness of the mind's processes (what we see, hear, taste, smell, feel, think, or intuit), and with awareness we notice our current state of mind (whether it is agitated, dull, alert, or distracted).

By practicing meditation and mindfulness, children and teens develop steady, flexible attention that's capable of shifting between different types of activity. They learn to move attention from their homework to a ringing phone and back again, for example, or from their thoughts to a physical sensation or to a task. On its own, mindful attention doesn't necessarily prioritize one type of activity over another, but it does require older children and teens to exercise a developmentally appropriate degree of awareness with respect to where their attention is focused and the quality of their attention; specifically, when kids are being mindful, they notice what their minds are doing and their states of mind. In a 2015 paper from the Center for Healthy Minds at the University of Wisconsin–Madison, Cortland Dahl and his colleagues explain that the term *meta-awareness* is used in scientific literature to describe the process of noticing. Without meta-awareness, they write, "we may be aware of the objects of attention, yet unaware of the processes of thinking, feeling and perceiving." Let's say a teenager who sits in front of an electronic device, checked out and bleary eyed, is highly focused and absorbed in what she's doing, but she's not noticing what she's doing. Hence, there's no meta-awareness, and from the perspective of mindfulness, she's lost. When sharing mindfulness with kids, it's important to remember that meta-awareness—noticing what their minds are doing and their current states of mind—is outside of many children's developmental ballparks. Dr. Mark Greenberg, Founding Director of the Prevention Research Center for the Promotion of Human Health at Pennsylvania State University and author of the pioneering social and emotional learning curriculum PATHS program explains that it's not likely young children are developmentally ready to understand or practice meta-awareness: "Exactly when these skills first develop depends on the child, but they're unlikely to develop before the fourth grade." Children who haven't yet developed the capacity for meta-awareness can still benefit greatly from mindful games that develop focused attention, self-regulation, and kindness, however.

Internal and external transformation is the ultimate goal of mindfulness and meditation; when children change their minds for the better, they're able to speak, act, and relate with more wisdom and compassion. Here's what this transformation looks like in the context of family life: through the practice of mindfulness and meditation, kids glean insights and life skills that foster **attention, balance,** and **compassion**—what I call **the ABCs.** While not an entirely linear progression, it's helpful to view these three qualities as developing sequentially, starting with attention, leading to emotional balance, and culminating with compassion. Their development is modest but meaningful at first and grows stronger over time. Steady, flexible attention develops kids' capacity to **Focus** and **Quiet** themselves; emotional balance enhances their capacity to **See** and **Reframe;** while speaking, acting, and relating to others (and themselves) with compassion develops their capacity to **Care** and **Connect.**

Perhaps the greatest impediment to change is that it's hard for kids to see their own minds clearly and directly. That's why the road to transformation starts with the development of concentration—a necessary tool for children's academic, emotional, and social toolboxes. If children and teenagers have the capacity to control their attention, they can use it to steady themselves even if the situation they're in is chaotic. With steady, flexible attention, the static in their minds can clear, and that's no small accomplishment. A clear head allows kids to see the changing, complex, and sometimes contradictory web of causes and conditions that lead to every moment. This is a simple process that is not always easy—especially when emotions run high—through which older children and teens can glean insight into what contemplatives have long taught: when they view their lives with wisdom and compassion, they're also connected to their values and ethics.

Young children who are not yet developmentally ready to exercise the level of cognitive control required for meta-awareness (who are not yet able to notice what their minds are doing in real time, together with their current state of mind) frequently embody an innate quality that's like mindfulness, in which they're fully engaged in the present with wonder and excitement—for example, when they are happy and content watching butterflies hover over a garden or ducks swimming in a pond. Sadly, the stress and strain of workaday life drums this spirited engagement in the natural world out of many children long before they become parents. The difference between how parents see the world given our pressure-cooker lives and the joyful wonder that children experience when they tap into the present moment is deftly illustrated in a picture book about a mother and her son hurrying to catch a train. In *Wait* by Antoinette Portis, a busy mom misses one ordinary, yet extraordinary, experience after another while her son delights in them—he vibes with a dachshund, waves to a construction worker, holds out a finger for a butterfly to land on, and tastes raindrops on his tongue. When they reach the station, the sight of a glorious spectacle stops both mother and son in their tracks. They let the train leave without them and stand on the platform together to marvel at a double rainbow. We don't need a double rainbow for the beauty of the moment to reveal itself, though. It's as close as our compost heaps, our laundry hampers, our dirty dishes, and the dinners that are cooking on our stoves. Even when we're stuck in a slow line at the DMV or ready to leave the house but can't head out until our partner, child, or both are ready too, we can find the joy and happiness that's always here by waiting with awareness.

mindful waiting

While we're waiting, we choose a nearby object to focus on (a potted plant, a coffee pot, the horizon). We gently gaze at the object in order to relax and notice what's happening within and around us.

LIFE SKILLS Focusing, Caring   TARGET AGES All Ages

LEADING THE GAME

1. Sit or stand comfortably, relax, and feel your breathing.
2. Choose something nearby that is pleasant to look at and rest your gaze on it. Keep your eyes soft and lightly focused on the object.
3. Notice any changes in your surroundings (colors, sounds, changes in light).
4. Sometimes you'll have thoughts, and sometimes you won't. When thoughts come, let them be. If you don't focus on them too much, they'll stay a while and leave on their own.

5. If you notice you're distracted, that means you know where your mind is. Congratulations, that's mindful awareness! Just return to gazing softly at the object.

6. *Talking points: What did you see? Were you surprised by what you saw? Did your surroundings stay the same? Did they change? How did you feel at first? How did you feel later? Did the time pass slowly or quickly?*

TIPS

1. When leading this exercise with young children, ask them to tell you what object they chose before moving to the next step.

2. This is a great game for the family to play when stuck in traffic, waiting for an appointment, or standing in line.

3. *Mindful Waiting* helps children calm themselves when they feel overly excited or upset.

Mindful games that give the present moment top billing bring parents back to the here and now of a child's world. They remind us that when we **Focus** on this very moment, what seem to be ordinary occurrences can become extraordinary occurrences that bring us joy. Vietnamese monk, poet, and peace activist Thich Nhat Hanh, who has been widely celebrated for his work sharing mindfulness with children and families, explains in the magazine *Mindful*:

> *When you contemplate the big, full sunrise, the more mindful and concentrated you are, the more the beauty of the sunrise is revealed to you. Suppose you are offered a cup of tea, very fragrant, very good tea. If your mind is distracted, you cannot really enjoy the tea. You have to be mindful of the tea, you have to be concentrated on it, so it can reveal its fragrance and wonder to you. That is why mindfulness and concentration are such sources of happiness. That's why a good practitioner knows*

how to create a moment of joy, a feeling of happiness at any time of the day.

Mindfulness develops concentration (or **Focus**), and it's no coincidence that Thich Nhat Hanh identifies mindfulness *and* concentration as prerequisites to discovering the happiness and joy that's hidden in every moment. Dr. Jack Kornfield, a leading American meditation teacher and cofounder of Spirit Rock Meditation Center, artfully describes the connection between concentration, happiness, and joy in his book *The Wise Heart*: "A peaceful heart gives birth to love. . . . When love meets happiness it turns to joy."

Prepare for the next game by finding a comfortable place to eat. Choose a simple food that can be eaten one at a time (grapes, blueberries, raisins) and place a few in a cup. For a special treat, use a square of chocolate or a Hershey's Kiss and challenge the children to keep the chocolate in their mouths until it melts completely. Ask them to pay attention to all five senses: *seeing* the chocolate, *hearing* the foil as it is removed, *tasting*, *smelling*, and *feeling* the chocolate in their mouths.

one bite at a time

We slowly eat one bite at a time in order to relax, enjoy, and appreciate the moment.

LIFE SKILLS Focusing, Caring   TARGET AGES All Ages

LEADING THE GAME
1. Pick up the food and notice what it looks like, feels like, and smells like. Notice your thoughts and how you feel while you're holding the food before you eat it.

2. Pop the food in your mouth for a moment, but don't chew it. Instead, notice what it feels like on your tongue. Is your mouth watering?

3. Now, chew it slowly and finally swallow it. Pay careful attention to how each step feels.

4. *Talking points: What was it like to hold the food in your mouth but not eat it? How did your mouth feel while chewing? How did your throat feel when swallowing? Did you notice any thoughts or emotions?*

TIPS

1. One way to describe this activity to younger children is "eating in slow motion."

2. Ask children if anything surprised them about how they felt. (Children will often notice saliva forming, a rumbling tummy, or a feeling of excitement.)

3. To help children eat less reflexively and with more awareness, ask them to notice how they feel before and after they eat. Here are some talking points: *How hungry do you feel? How full do you feel? Is there a difference between feeling hungry and feeling full? Have you ever felt full, but eaten anyway? Do you always eat when you feel hungry?*

As parents, many of us can relate to the mom in the story *Wait*, who is so focused on rushing to the train that she entirely misses the fun that her son is having in the moment. It appears that we're in the majority. In a study led by Drs. Matt Killingsworth and Daniel Gilbert at Harvard University, researchers used an app to randomly ask people what they were thinking and feeling. People reported that their minds wandered away from what they were doing about half the time and that they were happier when they were focused on a task than when they were distracted. I wasn't surprised to learn that people were happier when they focused on the present as a general rule, but I was surprised that this held true even when the task that they were focusing on was unpleasant. Dr. Susan Smalley, a UCLA professor emeritus and cofounder of the university's Mindful Awareness Research Center, pointed out that, in this study, people's minds wandered toward pleasant thoughts only about a third of the time. Given that two-thirds of people's mind wandering was toward unpleasant or neutral thoughts, it makes sense that being engaged in the present trumped mind wandering.

That doesn't necessarily mean, however, that a wandering mind always leads to unhappiness. Mind wandering and daydreaming play important roles in the development of critical thinking and problem solving. When children and teens imagine how various choices and outcomes might make them feel, their daydreaming can nurture self-awareness. When kids imagine how different choices and outcomes might make other people feel, their daydreaming can also nurture empathy. "Truly creative solutions to tough problems are often found by following a wandering path," writes Stanford University professor and neuroendocrinologist Dr. Robert Sapolsky in the *Wall Street Journal*, and "distraction makes tedium more tolerable." Not all mind wandering and daydreaming are alike, however, nor are they always helpful. Even when daydreaming is at its best—a highly creative, relaxing, and uplifting experience— there are times that children need to disengage from a daydream and return to the task at hand.

Which brings me to the relationship between daydreaming and mindfulness. When older kids daydream, they let go of trying to track what's happening in their heads and allow their minds to roam freely. In some meditation methods, older children and teens let their minds roam freely, too. But the difference between meditation and daydreaming is meta-awareness; older kids are tracking what's happening in their minds while they meditate, but not while they're daydreaming. So, for instance, if a teenager knows she's daydreaming while she's daydreaming, is she still daydreaming? If she's tracking what's happening in her head, she might be meditating, but she's probably not daydreaming. What happens if a teenager's mind starts to roam freely while she's meditating and she gets absorbed in her imagination? Is she still meditating? Nope. Mind wandering is not necessarily a problem, but if she's not aware that her mind is wandering, she's lost her mindfulness and is probably daydreaming. The moment she realizes that she's daydreaming, mindfulness can resume.

Scientists have yet to agree on one definition of daydreaming or of mindfulness, but they have reached a consensus on something else: spending some amount of time engaged in *positive, constructive daydreaming*, which is characterized by playful, wishful imagery and planful, creative thought, enhances learning and is good for kids' developing brains. Where does that leave parents with respect to mindfulness and daydreaming? There's no pat answer, other than that we need to help our children gauge how best to balance the two.

Part Three

Focusing

A few words can pack an enormous punch. One of my favorite children's stories is *The Carrot Seed*, a 1945 classic written by Ruth Krauss and illustrated by Crockett Johnson. A young boy's entire family discourages him from planting a carrot seed. On separate pages his mother and father tell him they're worried it won't come up. His older brother is certain that it won't come up. For four more of this book's twelve pages nothing happens, even though the little farmer weeds and waters his garden. "And then, one day," writes Krauss, "a carrot came up just as the little boy had known it would." When the boy's hard work pays off, we marvel at his determination and unflappable faith. We cheer when the carrot tops push through the earth and again when he wheels away a root vegetable that's bigger than he is. In about a hundred words, this little boy shows readers what the themes of patience and wise confidence look like in action—two qualities kids need for their attention to grow strong, steady, and flexible.

Children and their parents develop steady, flexible attention through brief but frequent periods of introspection, periods that might seem modest at first. "Practice a short time, many times," says Yongey Mingyur Rinpoche, and "like drops of water that fall into a big empty container one by one—drip-by-drip—eventually that big empty container will become full." This approach is not just a good one; it's the skillful one, especially when sharing mindfulness with youth. And it's an approach that requires patience and wise confidence. In *Real Happiness*, a leading meditation teacher and cofounder of the Insight Meditation Society, Sharon Salzberg, explains, "Imagine you're trying to split a huge piece of wood with a small axe. You hit that piece of wood ninety-nine times and nothing happens. Then you hit it the hundredth time and it splits open. You might wonder after that hundredth whack, what did I do differently that time? Did I hold the axe differently, did I stand differently? Why did it work the hundredth time and not the other ninety-nine? But, of course, we needed all those earlier attempts to weaken the fiber of the wood. It doesn't feel very good when we're only on hit number thirty-four or thirty-five; it seems as if we aren't making any progress at all. But we are."

To keep whacking at that wood until it splits takes patience and wise confidence, like that modeled by the boy in *The Carrot Seed* and by a little blue engine from another classic children's book of the same era, *The Little Engine That Could*, written by Arnold Munk, under the pen name Watty Piper. The little blue engine is way too small to haul a big train full of toys up a mountain, yet he digs in and starts to pull. All the way up the mountain he says, "I think I can, I think I can, I think I can," and all the way down he says, "I thought I could, I thought I could, I thought I could." Both archetypal picture books were written when daily life was slower than it is now. With much faster-paced lives, can today's children embody patience and wise confidence, like these beloved characters? I think they can if they focus more on the goodness of what they are doing, rather than on the result.

MINDFUL BREATHING

The first time I tried to meditate, I was with my husband and a group of strangers at the Zen Center of New York City. After a few minutes of sitting cross-legged on a cushion and staring at a white wall, my thoughts overpowered me, and I dashed out of the Zendo as if my hair was on fire. Looking back, I now understand why I couldn't sit still. My family was going through a rough patch, and it was simply too scary and painful for me to look inside myself for very long. I returned to meditation later, when the stressful events that had brought me there had calmed down.

Unfortunately, the mom who shared this next story with me did not. A bright working mother told me she approached meditation the same way she approached anything new—she read some books, listened to some audio recordings, and downloaded an app. Having done her research, she felt prepared and started to practice on her own. Yet every time she settled in to meditate, she was flooded by feelings of fear and helplessness. She had turned to meditation to help her steer through life's challenges, but no matter what technique she used or how hard she tried, this mom never felt calm, relaxed, or peaceful when she practiced. Instead, she felt agitated and overwhelmed. This is just one of many stories I've heard from people who stopped meditating because they found it to be frustrating.

Many children think meditation is easy, while most parents find it to be challenging at first. A professional, middle-aged dad told me that he had asked a young mindfulness teacher for meditation instructions in plain, easy-to-understand language. She suggested that he carve out five or ten minutes every day to sit comfortably or lie down and focus on his breathing. When thoughts came to mind, she told him to ignore them and go back to focusing on his breath. Although he remembered her instructions, he couldn't follow them. When his mind got busy, he was sucked into a mental loop of analyzing his problems. When he wasn't thinking, he'd get bored and zone out. Either way, this hopeful new meditator didn't feel that his time was well spent. When he was thinking and meditating, he figured he'd be better off sitting at his desk, and when he zoned out while meditating, he figured he'd be better off daydreaming on a chaise lounge in the backyard.

The mom who stopped meditating because she was overwhelmed by strong feelings, and the dad who stopped meditating because he got lost in thought or zoned out are just two of many people who've told me that they were drawn to meditation because they wanted to fix something in their lives that seemed broken—a similar pathway to the one that I took decades ago. Imagine my surprise when meditation turned the very notion of self-improvement on its head. Trading perfectionism for being more present with friends, family, and colleagues was an eye-opener for me, and I caught a glimpse of psychological freedom. In *The Wisdom of No Escape*, Pema Chödrön, one of the foremost American teachers of Tibetan

Buddhism, writes, "When people start to meditate or to work with any kind of spiritual discipline, they often think that somehow they're going to improve, which is a sort of subtle aggression against who they really are. It's a bit like saying, 'If I jog, I'll be a much better person.'" She continues, "Meditation practice isn't about trying to throw ourselves away and become something better. It's about befriending who we are already." Being our own best friend requires a shift in perspective away from self-improvement and toward acceptance of what's happening within and around us.

When we accept that strong, painful feelings, like restlessness, fear, anger, and sadness, will show up from time to time, we normalize uncomfortable feelings and learn that we can tolerate them. For children, this shift in perspective looks something like this: "It's really hard to sit still right now, and that's OK. Everyone feels that way sometimes. I can sit here and feel my body, feel all the energy I have—my heart beating fast, my legs and hands wanting to move—and I can take a breath, listen to sounds, and become curious about how I feel and how my feelings change, and I'll be OK."

Many contemplative traditions start meditation training with mindful breathing, and some of them end there. It's a remarkably simple and profound practice that's not always easy to do. In the next game, *Mindful Breathing*, kids relax and focus on the physical sensation of their breath as it moves in and out of their bodies. Children don't deliberately change the pace or intensity of their breathing, as they do when they breathe on purpose; instead, they allow their breathing to ebb and flow naturally. In *Living Beautifully*, Pema Chödrön explains, "The breath goes out and dissolves into space, then we breathe in again. This continues without any need to make it happen or control it. Each time the breath goes out, we simply let it go. Whatever occurs—our thoughts or emotions or sounds or movement in the environment—we train in accepting it without any value judgments." For children and teenagers, noticing and accepting the thoughts, feelings, and sensations that happen within them, along with the noises, movements, and distractions that happen outside of them, looks something like this:

My term paper is due tomorrow; I'll never finish it in time. OK, that's just thinking. I'm breathing in, I'm breathing out. It makes me mad that I wasn't invited to my friend's birthday party. OK, that's thinking, too. Breathing in, breathing out. I can't meditate with all the noise in the hallway. Thinking. OK. I'm breathing in, I'm breathing out, I'm breathing in, I'm breathing out. My nose itches. That's a sensation, but I'm going to label everything that comes to mind "thinking." In, out, in, out. My thoughts have started to slow down. Shoot, that's more thinking! In, out, in, out, in. I can't believe it! I've stopped thinking about my breathing! Argh, I'm thinking again. OK, label it "thinking." I'm breathing in, I'm breathing out.

mindful breathing

We pay close attention to the feeling of breathing to help us relax and rest in the moment.

LIFE SKILLS Focusing   TARGET AGES All Ages

LEADING THE GAME

1. Lie on your back with your legs flat on the floor and your arms by your sides. If you like, you can close your eyes.
2. Feel the back of your head touching the floor; now feel your shoulders against the floor; feel your upper back, arms, hands, lower back, legs, and feet.
3. Now notice what it feels like to breathe in and out. There's no right or wrong way to breathe—it doesn't matter if your breathing is fast or slow, deep or shallow.

4. Notice where you feel your breathing most. Do you feel the air going in and out just beneath your nose? Do you feel your belly moving up and down? Do you feel your lungs filling with air?
5. Pick the strongest of these sensations and pay careful attention to that area for a few breaths.
6. Now try paying close attention to your inhale. Can you notice the very moment you start to breathe in and then follow the feeling of your inhale all the way to the *very first moment* of your out-breath? If it's hard to keep your mind on your inhale, silently say the word "in" every time you breathe in.
   Let children try this for a minute or two.
7. Can you notice the very moment you begin to breathe out and then follow the feeling of your exhale all the way to the very first moment of your in-breath? If it's hard to keep your mind on your exhale, silently say the word "out" every time you breathe out.
   Let children try this for a few breaths.
8. Let's put it together and pay attention to an entire breath, carefully following every moment. If it's hard to keep your mind on your breathing, silently say the word "in" every time you breathe in and the word "out" every time you breathe out.
   Let children try this for a few breaths.
9. Let's check how our bodies feel now. Feel the back of your head touching the floor; now feel your shoulders against the floor; feel your upper back, arms, hands, lower back, legs, and feet.
10. When you're ready, open your eyes and sit up slowly to finish. Take a breath and notice how you feel.

TIPS

1. Lying down is often children's favorite meditation posture, but *Mindful Breathing* can also be practiced sitting or standing.
2. If it's difficult for kids to stay still when they practice *Mindful Breathing* while sitting or standing, they often find it helpful to sway from side to side slowly and with control.

3. Given the wide range of information kids process every moment, it's no wonder that narrowing their field of attention to focus on the sensation of breathing can be difficult to do. That's why these instructions include a strategy that's been used by meditators for generations: when it's hard to focus on your breathing, silently say the word "in" when you breathe in and "out" when you breathe out.

4. Give children and teenagers an opportunity to talk about their feelings and experiences after leading *Mindful Breathing* (or any introspective activity). Check-ins can range from a few words from each person to a full discussion.

5. From time to time, have children check and see if their bodies are tense, and encourage them to relax.

Resting a light pillow (or other soft object that has a little heft to it) on new meditators' bellies helps them **Focus** on the sensation of breathing. In the next game, young children place a stuffed animal on their tummies and pretend that they're rocking it to sleep with the up and down movements of their breathing. For older children or teens, substitute a pillow, cushion, or other soft, weighted object for the stuffed animal.

rock-a-bye

We pretend to rock a stuffed animal to sleep on our bellies to relax our bodies and quiet our minds. As we breathe in, the animal rocks up; as we breathe out, the animal rocks back down.

LIFE SKILLS Focusing   TARGET AGES Young Children (with a modification for Older Children and Teens)

1. Lie on your back with your legs flat on the floor and your arms by your sides. If you like, you can close your eyes. Now I'm going to place a stuffed animal on your belly.
2. Feel the back of your head touching the floor. Now feel your shoulders, upper back, arms, hands, lower back, legs, and feet. You can pat the stuffed animal on your tummy and notice what that feels like, too.
3. Now notice what it feels like to breathe in and out, moving the animal up and down with your breathing. How does your body feel? Is your mind busy?
   Wait about one to three minutes before moving to the next instruction.
4. If it's hard to keep your mind on your breathing, silently say the word "up" every time the animal moves up and silently say the word "down" every time the animal moves down.
5. Let's check how our bodies feel now. Feel the back of your head touching the floor; now feel your shoulders against the floor; feel your upper back, arms, hands, lower back, legs, and feet.
6. When you're ready, open your eyes and sit up slowly to finish. Take a breath and notice how you feel. Do you feel different than you felt before?

Minds are designed for thinking, yet thinking has a way of distracting meditators with stories about their pasts and futures. Counting is often used as an anchor for new meditators' attention because it takes advantage of their innate tendency to think while narrowing what they're thinking about to a single word. Counting is a familiar strategy to quiet busy minds outside of meditation circles, too. People who suffer from insomnia have long been encouraged to count sheep or count backwards when they have trouble falling asleep. The contemplative scholar Dr. Alan Wallace, author of many books on mindfulness and meditation, including *Genuine Happiness: Meditation as the Path to Fulfillment*, calls counting breaths "training wheels for meditation" because counting keeps a meditator's mind occupied until her thoughts slow and can settle down.

counting breaths

We count breaths to develop concentration. Just like playing a sport or an instrument, the more we practice, the better we are at concentrating.

LIFE SKILLS Focusing   TARGET AGES All Ages

LEADING THE GAME

1. Sit with your back straight and body relaxed, resting your hands gently on your knees.
2. Breathe in naturally and silently say, "One" in your mind. Then relax your forehead as you breathe out.
   Raise one finger and wait for everyone to breathe in and out.
3. Let's do it again. Breathe in naturally and silently say, "Two" in your mind. Then relax your neck and shoulders as you breathe out.
   Raise two fingers.
4. Now breathe in and silently say, "Three" in your mind and relax your tummy as you breathe out.
   Raise three fingers.
5. Let's try it again, but this time I'm not going to talk. Sync your breath to my hand motions, counting silently on your own. Don't forget to relax as you breathe out.
6. *Talking points: Did your mind get quiet when you were counting breaths? Did you feel relaxed? How long did it take? Did your mind get busy again, or did it stay quiet?*

1. Young children who aren't ready to count in their heads can count breaths with their fingers. Ask them to sync their movements with yours as you hold up one, two, and three fingers.

2. The whole family can trade off leading three breaths at the kitchen table. The first person starts, silently leading three breaths by holding up one, then two, and finally three fingers. Whoever is sitting to this person's right picks up the count by holding up one finger and leading the next series of three breaths. This continues around the table until everyone has had a turn.

3. Encourage kids to experiment with counting on the in-breath to help them feel energized and alert or on the out-breath to help them feel relaxed and calm.

4. For some older children, teens, and parents, it can be helpful to count from one to ten (rather than one to three) and others find that counting to a smaller number is more effective. Try each one to see what works best for you.

5. You can also count, "One, one, one" on the inhale:

   • Ask children to silently say, "One, one, one . . ." for as long as they breathe in. Ask them to relax as they exhale.

   • Repeat by having them silently count, "Two, two, two . . ." Again ask them to relax as they exhale.

   • Continue this exercise for up to ten breaths.

   • Try counting, "One, one, one" on the exhale rather than the inhale.

The following game includes a movement sequence that playfully develops young children's self-awareness by giving them a felt sense of their bodies in relationship to nearby people and objects. Here are a couple of tips to keep in mind before you lead the game: It's helpful to have a picture of a grandfather clock handy to show young children what a pendulum looks like; and, the instructions are written with the children sitting on the floor, but kids can also play *Tick Tock* standing or sitting in a chair.

tick-tock

We sway from side to side, like a pendulum on a clock, while chanting a rhyme. This game helps us develop body awareness and practice moving our bodies with control.

LIFE SKILLS Focusing TARGET AGES Young Children

LEADING THE GAME

1. *Talking points: What sound does a clock make? Does anyone know what a grandfather clock is? Does anyone know what a pendulum is?*
2. Now we're going to practice swaying side to side like the pendulum of a grandfather clock. Sit with your back straight and your body relaxed, resting your hands on the floor at your sides.
3. Let's all raise our right hands together. Put your hand on the floor next to you and lean your body to the right. Now push your body to the left and catch your weight with your left hand on the floor. And now rock back to the right hand again. Can you feel your body moving right, center, and left?
4. Now let's say, "Tick-tock" as we sway from side to side. "Tick-tock, tick-tock . . ."
5. We're going to stop swaying soon, so let's all say this rhyme together: "Tick—tock—like a—clock—until—I find—my center—STOP."
6. Let's end just like we started, with backs straight and bodies relaxed. Rest your hands on your knees and take a few breaths.

1. *Counting Breaths* with hand gestures is a fun and effective way to extend *Tick-Tock*. After children say "stop," hold up one finger. Everyone takes one breath. Hold up a second finger, and everyone takes another breath. Everyone takes a third breath when you hold up a third finger.

2. Another popular extension to *Tick-Tock* is *Fading Tone*, a mindful listening game for young children that comes later in the book.

3. You can also rock back and forth to the beat of a drum.

— 7 —

SPOTLIGHT OF ATTENTION

We often tell kids to "pay attention" without explaining what we mean or teaching them how. Why? Because adults often don't know much about how attention works; and even when we understand attention intellectually, we often haven't tried to develop it purposely. That's where mindfulness and meditation can help. It doesn't take long on the cushion to learn firsthand that mindfulness develops two ways of paying attention that are remarkably useful: a focused one that helps us concentrate, manage distractions, and accomplish an immediate objective; plus a more open, receptive one that's the source of playfulness, creativity, and emotional regulation.

Borrowing from contemplative scholar and author Andrew Olendzki's contribution to the *Clinical Handbook of Mindfulness*, I refer to these two ways of paying attention as the *spotlight of attention* and the *floodlight of attention*. The spotlight of attention is a clear, stable, narrow beam that lights up a single object. In meditation, that object is called an *anchor*, and games that ask kids to focus on an anchor to the exclusion of all else are called *anchor games*. The anchor can be one thing (a flower) or a group of things (a bouquet). The floodlight of attention is a wide, receptive beam that lights

up a broad field of changing experience. Games that use the floodlight of attention are called *awareness games*. We'll explore anchor games in this chapter and awareness games in chapter 11.

The spotlight of attention allows children to remain alert, undistracted, and focused. Since children also remain alert, undistracted, and focused when they use the floodlight of attention, these two ways of paying attention are not entirely separate, although it's helpful to explain them this way. Pioneering meditation teacher Chögyam Trungpa Rinpoche, one of the first to translate Tibetan Buddhist concepts into secular terms and bring them to the West, taught that the spotlight of attention (undistracted, alert, and focused attention) is 25 percent of the floodlight of attention; thus, without the spotlight there could be no floodlight.

Both ways of paying attention are regulated by a set of interrelated neural networks known as *executive function*, which control goal-oriented behavior from the "top down." In other words, processing information from the head first, as opposed to "bottom-up" processing that starts with physical sensations. The neural networks that regulate executive function are made stronger through **Focusing**. Just as lifting weights is a physical exercise that makes muscles stronger, **Focus** is a mental exercise that develops new neural pathways and strengthens existing ones. This is an example of the theme cause and effect and of something scientists call *neuroplasticity*—the capacity of neurons and the neural networks in the brain to change in response to experiences. Neuroscientists often describe neuroplasticity by saying, "Neurons that fire together wire together"; in other words, the more kids work a specific neural network, the greater the effect. Executive function is highly predictive of children's academic, social, and emotional success and is responsible for core skills that children use all the time—for instance, remembering information, self-regulating, noticing, and shifting attention. When seemingly simple kids' games—like Freeze Tag, Head, Shoulders, Knees, and Toes, and Simon Says—require children to pay attention, remember rules, and exhibit control, kids are developing these core executive skills.

Research on children and teenagers is still in its infancy, but the studies that have been published suggest that mindfulness and meditation also develop executive functioning. One of the first studies to be published was of the Inner Kids program. Spearheaded by Dr. Susan Smalley and published in the *Journal of Applied School Psychology*, this randomized, control-group study looked at sixty-four second- and third-grade students in a classroom setting. In the *Handbook of Mindfulness and Education*, Drs. Brian Galla and David Black wrote (in a chapter that I also contributed to):

Children with lower initial self-regulation who participated in the Inner Kids training showed significant improvement in self-regulation following training compared to children in the control group. A similar pattern of change emerged for both teacher-reported and parent-reported self-regulation, suggesting that improvements in children's self-regulation generalized to non-school settings. Based on both teacher and parent reports, children with initial lower self-regulation who received training in Inner Kids showed significant improvement in their ability to initiate tasks, to shift between tasks, and to notice performance on tasks. Interestingly, improvements in these three domains may reflect the set of skills practiced during mindfulness training, which included focusing attention on a physical sensation (initiate), sustaining focus over time (notice), and redirecting attention back to the sensation following any lapses (shifting). While the results of this study are preliminary, they do provide interesting evidence that mindfulness training may be particularly beneficial for otherwise healthy youth who have relatively low self-regulatory abilities.

The anchor games in this chapter strengthen attention as kids **Focus** on an object, note when they become distracted, and shift their attention back to the object. Not surprisingly, when parents lead anchor games they frequently use the terms *anchor*, *concentration*, and *distraction*. It's helpful to define these terms up front by saying something like: "Your anchor is something that you choose to focus on and is here right now. Concentration is when you focus on your anchor. And distraction is when you pay attention to something else."

Drop the Monkeys is a remarkably useful visual demonstration of how kids work with the thoughts, emotions, and sensations that bubble up during anchor games. It is also a wonderful group facilitation tool that brings playfulness and a sense of humor to the check-ins that follow introspective practices. Using a children's toy called Barrel of Monkeys as a prop, children joke about the thoughts that grabbed their attention.

drop the monkeys

With the help of a colorful plastic toy, we build a chain of monkeys to demonstrate how we can notice thoughts and let them go.

LIFE SKILLS Focusing, Seeing
TARGET AGES Young Children, Older Children

LEADING THE DEMONSTRATION

1. *Talking points: Do you ever notice that instead of paying attention to what's happening in the moment, you become distracted by a thought about something that happened in the past or something that might happen in the future? What are some examples?*
2. In this game, each monkey represents a thought, emotion, or

sensation that has grabbed our attention.
Offer an example of a distracting thought and hold up a monkey.

3. Now you give me an example. For each distraction we think of, I'll add another monkey to the chain.
Take about three to four examples from children, and add a monkey to the chain for each example.

4. These are all monkeys we can let go of, right? We don't need any of these thoughts and emotions distracting us right now, so let's drop them.
Drop the monkey chain back into the plastic barrel.

5. That was fun. Let's try it again. Can you think of more examples?

TIPS

1. Although the barrel of monkeys is used more like a toy with younger children, it can be a helpful visual aid when working with older children (and adults!).

2. Extend the demonstration by adding a discussion at the end. Here are some talking points: *How often does your mind wander away from the present into the past or future? Do thoughts and emotions stay the same, or do they change over time?*

3. *Drop the Monkeys* helps children turn distractions into success stories. Hold up the monkey chain and ask children what to call the moment when they notice they're distracted. Kids shout, "Mindfulness!" because they know where their minds are at that instant.

4. Occasionally, children bring up a serious topic that merits further inquiry. If the timing and venue are right, there's no better time to talk about what's bothering them. But sensitive topics are sometimes raised at inappropriate times. If that happens, acknowledge the topic and the child's concern, then shift the tone and subject matter of the discussion. Be sure to revisit the topic with the child privately at a more appropriate time and place.

Next, young meditators choose a breathing anchor by noticing where they feel their breath most easily—near their noses, in their chests, or inside their bellies.

choose your breathing anchor

We pay attention to the feeling of breathing where we notice it most—near the nose, chest, or belly—to help us relax and focus on the present moment.

LIFE SKILLS Focusing   TARGET AGES All Ages

LEADING THE GAME

1. Sit with your back straight and your body relaxed, resting your hands gently on your knees, and close your eyes if you're comfortable. Notice what it feels like to breathe in and out right now.
2. Place one finger under your nose and feel your breath going in and out. Can you feel it?
3. Next, place your hand on your chest, above your heart. Can you feel your hand moving when you breathe?
4. Now place your hand on your belly and feel the movement of your breathing there.
5. Put your hands back on your knees and breathe naturally. Notice where you feel the movement of your breath most easily. Is it just beneath your nose, at your chest, or at your belly?

6. Now I'm going to ask you to make a choice and focus on your breathing where you feel it most. Wherever that is, that's the place I'll be talking about when I use the word "anchor." We're going to use this anchor for the rest of the game, so if you need to check again to see where it's easiest to feel your breathing right now, go ahead.

7. Great. Let's try this for a few more breaths together. See if you can keep your body relaxed and lightly rest your attention on your anchor at the same time. This is how we rest in the feeling of the movement of our breath.

TIPS

1. *Choose Your Breathing Anchor* can also be practiced lying down or standing.

2. When leading more than one child, ask them to put one hand on their head when they've chosen an anchor. Wait for everyone to choose an anchor before you continue.

3. It can be helpful to start the activity with a relaxing body scan. For example, "Feel your eyelids closed, feel your shoulders relaxed, feel your hands touching your knees, feel your legs touching the floor or the chair . . ."

4. When children have had some practice sitting for longer periods, you can extend this activity with a few minutes of *Mindful Breathing*.

5. To vary the game, ask children to choose another simple, neutral object to anchor their attention: a sound, a sensation, or counting, for example.

Another common anchor for attention is sound. In the next game, young children listen to a tone that starts out strongly and fades away. Like all anchor games, *Fading Tone* develops the life skill **Focus**, but it also introduces the theme "everything changes." At the end of the game, ask children, "What happened to the sound?"

fading tone

We listen closely to the sound of a tone as it fades away to help us relax and focus.

LIFE SKILLS Focusing   **TARGET AGES** Young Children, Older Children

LEADING THE GAME

1. Sit with your back straight and your body relaxed, resting your hands gently on your knees. If you like, you can close your eyes.
2. When I ring the bell, listen to the sound of the tone as it fades away. Raise your hand when you can't hear the tone anymore—when the sound stops.
3. I'll ring the bell a few more times. Sometimes the tone will be short, and sometimes it will be long. Pay close attention, so you can raise your hand as soon as you hear the sound stop.
4. *Talking points: What was it like to listen to the tone? How do you feel now? Does your body feel relaxed? Is your mind busy or quiet? What do you think happened to the sound after it faded—where did it go?*

TIPS

1. After the first round, you can repeat the game without verbal instruction:
   - Place your hand on your belly as if you're feeling your breathing— this prompts children to do the same and signals them that the game has begun. Wait until everyone is ready before continuing.
   - Strike the bell and put one hand to your ear, letting children know it's time to focus on the sound of the tone.
   - Children will raise their hands when they no longer hear the sound. Wait until all the children raise their hands before you continue. If necessary, raise your hand when the sound stops to cue the children to raise theirs.

- Repeat the sequence two more times (three times total).
2. *Fading Tone* is a terrific game to play sitting around the kitchen table.
3. Keep in mind that the children will hear the tone stop at different times.
4. *Fading Tone* is creative way to extend the game *Tick-Tock*. Ring the bell when children have found their center and are no longer swaying from side to side.
5. Here are several more ways to extend or vary this game:
   - Have children keep their eyes open. Place an object in front of them to focus on, like a smooth stone. If sitting in a circle, place the stone or other object in the center as a focal point.
   - Vary the length of the tone. Shorten the tone by dampening the bell with one hand or extend it by ringing the bell loudly. Extend the tone only for as long as children can comfortably concentrate; mute the bell if children get restless.
   - Ring the bell multiple times and ask children to count the number of tones they hear.
   - Add other sounds, using a tuning fork, shakers, or other instruments. Ask children how many different sounds they heard and to describe them. Later, have them guess what instruments they heard.

It's a lot to ask kids to stay still for a long time. That's why games that give kids a chance to stretch, shake, and synchronize movements are important—they're a fun, and incredibly useful, way to help children become attentive to the connection between their minds and their bodies. Playful awareness activities in which kids move in sync with one another help kids identify their physical boundaries; for example, in some games young children scoot in as close as possible to someone or something without touching. Movement games are also valuable when used to precede longer periods of meditation for older children and teenagers because they help kids settle down. There's more to mindfulness-based movement activities than giving kids a chance to move and stretch, however. They also help children develop self-regulation; give those who find it hard to stay still an opportunity to practice successfully; and give everybody a chance to release excess energy.

The next three activities are anchor games that involve movement and develop the spotlight of attention. In *Slow and Silent Walking*, kids anchor their attention on the sensations in their feet and legs as they step. Prepare by marking a starting and an ending point about six feet apart, with tape or objects. You'll signal children to start walking by ringing a bell. If you don't have a bell you can cue children verbally.

slow and silent walking

We walk slowly and purposefully. Every time we step, we feel the sensations in our feet and legs.

LIFE SKILLS Focusing   TARGET AGES All Ages

LEADING THE GAME

1. We're going to begin at one line and walk very slowly across the floor to the other line, feeling our feet touching the floor as we walk. Keep your gaze downward to make it easier to concentrate.
2. Let's get ready by standing on this line with our backs straight, knees soft, and muscles relaxed. When I ring the bell, we'll start walking very slowly.
   Ring the bell.
3. Notice the feeling in each foot as you step. Do you feel the heel of your foot, the ball of your foot, and your toes?

4. When we get to the other line, we'll slowly turn around and wait for the bell. That's the signal to start walking again. We'll focus on our breathing while you wait.

   Ring the bell again and continue for as long as children seem engaged.

TIPS

1. Although the instructions suggest tape and a bell, don't worry if you don't have these tools with you. Children can walk between any starting and ending point, and you can cue them to start walking with a clap, a snap of the fingers, or verbally.
2. Occasionally remind kids to notice the sensations in their feet and legs. This helps them stay on track and can also soothe those who feel unsettled or upset.
3. After some practice, have children pay attention to two parts of walking: Putting the foot down *and* lifting the foot up.
4. Later, have children pay attention to three parts of walking: Putting the foot down, lifting the foot up, and moving the leg forward.
5. Kids don't need the lines on the floor to mark their lanes, and once they understand the game they'll be ready to walk longer distances. For instance, they can walk in the hallway, across the room, or outside in nature.

Slow and Silent Walking builds kids' awareness of where and how they move through physical space—where their bodies are in relation to other people (arms, legs, hands, elbows) and things (tables, chairs, a vase), as well as the quality of their movements (sluggish, quick, fluid, jerky). The next two games also develop this aspect of self-awareness. In *Balloon Arms* children anchor their attention on the sensations they feel when they move their arms up and down or back and forth.

balloon arms

We practice focusing by slowly moving our arms up and down or back and forth, in sync with one another's movements.

LIFE SKILLS Focusing   TARGET AGES Young Children, Older Children

LEADING THE GAME

1. When you fill a balloon with air (inflate it) it gets bigger, and when you deflate it, the air comes out, and it gets smaller.
2. I'm going to move my hands up, like a balloon filling with air, then down, like a balloon getting smaller and deflating.
   Demonstrate by resting the palms of your hands on top of your head, with the tips of your fingers touching. Keeping your fingers together, raise your arms to mime a balloon inflating; then lower your arms to mime a balloon deflating.
3. Now sync your movements with mine. Pay close attention to the sensations in your arms, upper back, and neck as you move.
4. Great. Let's try it a few more times.

TIPS

1. Once children understand the game, have them lead the movement.
2. Try using a balloon as a visual aid.
3. Change the direction of the movement. Start with your hands on your chest and move your arms forward and back—away from your chest and back toward your heart.
4. You can also have children sync their movements with their breath (breathing in as the balloon inflates, breathing out as the balloon deflates). Be careful not to sync more than three or four breaths, as some children may begin to feel dizzy.

In the next game children develop **Focus** by moving slowly like a sloth. It's fun to use Eric Carle's children's book *"Slowly, Slowly, Slowly," Said the Sloth* to lead the game, but it can be played without the book by asking children to **Focus** on the changing sensations in their bodies as they slowly move one arm or leg. To prepare, make sure that children have enough space to move without knocking into anyone or anything.

slowly, slowly

We practice focusing by paying close attention to the sensations in our bodies as we move in slow motion.

LIFE SKILLS Focusing   TARGET AGES All Ages

LEADING THE GAME

1. Let's see what it's like to move very slowly. We're going to move in slow motion together like this.
   Demonstrate by moving your arm and describing the sensations in your shoulder, back, and neck as you move.
2. Are you ready? Make sure you have enough space around you so you won't bump into anyone or anything when you move.
3. Let's start by moving one leg slowly. Notice the feelings in your whole body as you move—not just the feelings in your leg.
4. Great! Slowly lower your leg. Now let's reach down in slow motion and touch the floor with our hands. Stay here for a moment, and notice if the sensations in your body change or stay the same.
5. Slowly stand up, and then move your head from side to side in slow motion. Notice the sensations in your neck when you move. Do you feel sensations in other parts of your body too? Now try it with your eyes closed. What does it feel like?

1. The games *Slowly, Slowly* and *Balloon Arms* are excellent ways for children to practice focusing while standing in line or transitioning between activities.

2. These two games also offer children the opportunity to lead, and to take turns leading, one another.

3. Here's how you can use Eric Carle's classic children's book *"Slowly, Slowly, Slowly," Said the Sloth* as a starting point to teach young children how to move in slow motion:

   - Explain that you're going to read a story that repeats the words "slowly, slowly, slowly" many times, and every time children hear those three words, they'll raise one arm in slow motion. Encourage them to pay close attention to the feelings in their arm, shoulder, back, and neck as they move.

   - Demonstrate the movement, and describe the sensations that you feel as you move your arm in slow motion. Then, read the story.

   - Raise your arm slowly every time you read the phrase "slowly, slowly, slowly," and children will mimic the movement.

   - Pause after Jaguar's question to the Sloth, "Why are you so lazy?" and ask children, "Do you think the Sloth is lazy because he moves slowly?" Wait for children to answer before turning the page to read the Sloth's response.

   - Move your arm in slow motion one last time when you read the words "slowly, slowly, slowly."

Children and parents are often introduced to meditation through mindful breathing, using the sensation of breathing as their anchor. Some find **Focusing** on their breathing to be easy, and others find it to be hard. And sometimes, those who like to use their breath as an anchor get bored with it or find that this method stops working for them. Experiences like these are to be expected and are why it's important to experiment with more than one anchor for attention. Movements, sensations, sounds, images, and words are all easily accessible anchors that develop **Focus**. Another common anchoring technique is to softly gaze at an object. When I first started sharing mindfulness with my son, we would sit on cushions and look at a yellow rubber duck. When he got bored, I swapped out the rubber duck for a bright green plastic frog. When he got older, we gazed at a smooth stone.

— 8 —

A PEACEFUL HEART

When children and teenagers practice visualization, they anchor their attention on an image in their heads and on the sensations that they associate with it. Because children are focusing on one thing to the exclusion of everything else, visualizations are anchor games that develop **Focus** and the spotlight of attention. The visualizations in this chapter are based on loving-kindness practices, a core element of the classical meditation canon. Loving-kindness adds a meaningful layer to anchor games by inspiring a deep appreciation for all living things while cultivating empathy and nurturing compassion.

imaginary hugs

We picture our family, our friends, and ourselves in a peaceful place where we are happy, healthy, and having fun.

LIFE SKILLS Focusing, Caring   TARGET AGES Young Children

1. *Talking points: What does it mean to pretend that you're doing something else or that you are someplace else? What does it feel like to hug someone you care about? If someone you'd like to hug isn't in the same room with you, can you give them an imaginary hug, anyway? Let's try it.*

2. Sit with your back straight and your body relaxed, resting your hands gently on your knees. Close your eyes, and let's take a few breaths together. I'll keep my eyes open and watch the room.

3. Imagine a peaceful place that you would like to visit with your friends and family. It can be a place you know (your back-yard), a place you know about but haven't visited yet (another country), or an imaginary place (the Hundred Acre Wood from *Winnie-the-Pooh*).

   When practicing with more than one child, ask children to put one hand on their heads when they've chosen a place. Wait until everyone has a peaceful place in mind before you continue.

4. Imagine that you can feel, see, touch, hear, taste, or smell something in your peaceful place. Maybe you smell delicious chocolate chip cookies baking in the oven or hear the sound of water splashing against the rocks in a waterfall.

5. Now, let's send friendly wishes to ourselves. Give yourself a big hug, imagine you're having fun in your peaceful place, and silently say to yourself something like: "I hope I have a great day. I hope I have lots of fun playing with my friends." You can use these wishes or choose other wishes and say them silently in your own words.

6. Next, we're going to give someone we love an imaginary hug. Make your arms into a circle in front of your chest and think of someone you'd like to hug. Imagine that he or she is with you in your peaceful place. Picture him or her smiling and imagine that you're hugging each other. Then silently say something like: "I hope you are happy and have a great day. I hope you have what you need."

7. Are there more people you'd like to hug and invite to your peaceful place? Open your arms wide enough so that everyone can fit. Picture all of them smiling and laughing and imagine you're giving everyone a group hug. Then silently send friendly wishes, like these: "I want all of you to be happy, healthy, and strong. I hope you have fun today and feel lots of love from your family and friends."

8. With arms stretched out wide, imagine that the whole planet is a peaceful place and that you are hugging the planet as you silently say: "I hope everyone is happy today. I want all of us to be healthy and safe and to feel peaceful and content." Remember, you can silently say these wishes or choose your own wishes and put them in your own words.

9. Now open your eyes. Reach your hands high up to the sky as you take a big breath in, and as you breathe out, lower your hands to your knees.

10. *Talking points: What did it feel like to give yourself a hug and to send yourself a friendly wish? How did it feel to give someone else an imaginary hug and send friendly wishes to them?*

TIPS

1. It's tough for children to picture something in their heads when their eyes are open; yet some kids are not comfortable closing their eyes, especially in a room full of people. That's why we suggest you mention that you'll keep your eyes open and watch the room.

2. When kids feel upset, they can soothe themselves with a hug. Add another self-soothing, sensory element to *Imaginary Hugs* by asking young children to pat themselves on the back to congratulate themselves for a job well done. They can do this before the game, for what they've they just completed—their homework or helping out in the kitchen—or else afterward, for practicing kindness by sending friendly wishes.

3. The check-in that follows this game is an opportunity to remind children of other sensory experiences they can use to soothe and

calm themselves: singing or listening to music (hearing); taking a bubble bath (feeling); slowly eating something delicious (tasting); walking in nature (seeing); or placing a hand on their hearts to feel their breathing (feeling).

Imaginary Hugs is my go-to game with young children for sending friendly wishes. When sharing kindness games with older children and teens, I start with the next visualization instead. Here's an important caution for parents to keep in mind when leading any kindness visualization: It's easy for children and teens to misinterpret these games as gentle nudges to change how they feel about a specific person or a group of people—in other words, for them to *like* someone they *don't like*. In practice, however, kindness visualizations don't ask kids to change their feelings, only to keep an open mind. Just as the appreciation games *Life Is Good* and *Three Good Things* develop a holistic mind-set that includes everyday blessings together with everyday challenges, kindness games invite kids to hold seemingly conflicting ideas in mind simultaneously. Before leading kindness visualizations, remind kids that there are plenty of healthy reasons not to like people and not to spend time with people whom they don't respect or who don't treat them well. What's important is that older children and teens remember that they can have more than one feeling about someone; they can wish someone well, even though they don't like or respect him or her.

Kindness visualizations can bring up strong emotions that feel overwhelming regardless of a meditator's age. It's better not to insist that a child or teenager send friendly wishes if they're not comfortable doing so, but it makes sense to suggest that they try a different game before moving on to something else. *Kindness with Every Step* is a good choice for kids who find kindness visualizations to be difficult or have a hard time staying still; *Wishes for the World* is a good alternative for young children; and sending friendly wishes to an adorable animal is another way to modify kindness games so that they are less challenging. If a child or teenager doesn't feel comfortable with any of these alternatives, that's OK; just move on to another activity, perhaps one of the relational mindfulness games that come later in the book.

friendly wishes

We imagine that everyone is happy, safe, healthy, and living in peace, in order to practice kindness and concentration.

LIFE SKILLS Focusing, Caring   TARGET AGES All Ages

LEADING THE GAME

1. Lie on your back with your legs flat on the floor and your arms by your sides. If you like, you can close your eyes.
2. Feel the back of your head resting against the floor or pillow; feel your arms and hands relaxing into the ground; feel your back, your legs, and your feet relaxing, too.
3. Now we're going to send some friendly wishes together. *Guide children through the following visualization (or something similar in your own words).*
4. Imagine that you feel happy. Imagine that you're smiling, laughing, and having fun. Even if you're not feeling happy right now, that's OK. Just imagine that you're laughing, playing with your friends, or doing something that you love to do.
5. Then silently say something like this: "I want to be happy and helpful today. I hope that I'm healthy and strong. I hope I feel peaceful and content. I want to feel lots of love." You can use these wishes or choose your own wishes and silently say them in your own words.

6. Now imagine that your wishes create a warm feeling that grows when you pay attention to it. Imagine the warm feeling starts near your heart. As you silently say the friendly wishes, the feeling reaches out to your fingers, toes, and the top of your head. This warm feeling fills up your whole body.

7. Imagine that this feeling has a color—it can be any color you want. Maybe it's blue, red, or yellow. Imagine this beautiful color has filled your whole body, and as it grows it spills out of your fingers, and your toes, and into the room.

8. Imagine that the other people in the room can feel this warm feeling and see this beautiful color, too. They're smiling and happy. Silently say to them: "I hope that you're strong and healthy. I want you to feel peaceful, safe, and content. I hope you have what you need and feel lots of love." Silently repeat these wishes or choose other wishes and put them into your own words.

9. Picture the cozy, warm feeling you're creating and imagine the beautiful color has grown so big that it's bursting out of the room. Imagine that the warm feeling keeps growing, and growing, until it reaches everyone and everything on the planet. Imagine that everyone you want to feel your friendly wishes can feel them. Picture them smiling because they sense that you're wishing them well. Silently say: "I hope you're happy and have what you need. I hope you feel strong and healthy. I hope you feel loved, valued, and taken care of. I hope you feel content." You can use these wishes or choose your own wishes and say them in your own words.

10. When you're ready, open your eyes and feel your body against the floor again. Sit up slowly to finish. Take a breath and notice how you feel.

11. *Talking points: Name some wishes that you'd like to send to other people, to the planet, and to yourself. How do you feel when you send friendly wishes?*

1. In the earlier section on **Quieting**, kids considered different ways that their minds affect their bodies and their bodies affect their minds. You can extend these conversations to kindness visualizations by asking if children notice a difference between how they feel before and how they feel after they send friendly wishes.

The next game for young children encourages empathy and compassion. It starts as a concentration game that develops **Focus**, using breath as an anchor, and becomes a kindness visualization that develops **Focus** by using a mental image as an anchor. Make sure to have stuffed animals or other soft, slightly weighted objects, like pillows, bean bags, or cushions, to place on the children's tummies.

rock-a-bye with friendly wishes

We pretend to rock a stuffed animal to sleep on our bellies to relax our bodies and quiet our minds. As we breathe in, the animal rocks up; as we breathe out, the animal rocks back down.

LIFE SKILLS Focusing, Caring   TARGET AGES Young Children (with a modification for Older Children and Teens)

LEADING THE GAME

1. Lie on your back with your legs flat on the floor and your arms by your sides. If you like, you can close your eyes. Now I'm going to place a stuffed animal on your belly.
   For older children or teens, you may substitute a pillow, cushion, or other soft, weighted object.
2. Feel the back of your head touching the floor. Now feel your shoulders, upper back, arms, hands, lower back, legs, and feet. You can pat

the stuffed animal on your tummy and notice what that feels like, too.

3. Now notice what it feels like to breathe in and out, moving the animal up and down with your breathing. Does anything change in your mind and body when you rest like this?
   Wait about one to three minutes before moving to the next instruction.

4. If it's hard to focus on your breathing, silently say the word "up" every time your stuffed animal moves up and silently say the word "down" every time your stuffed animal moves down.

5. Check how your body feels now. Feel the back of your head touching the floor; now feel your shoulders against the floor; feel your upper back, arms, hands, lower back, legs, and feet.

6. We'll end by sending friendly wishes. Let's start with ourselves. Silently say these wishes, or you can choose other wishes and say them in your own words: "I'd like to be happy, helpful, and strong today. I hope I have fun with my friends and my family."

7. Next, picture someone you would like to wish well, and when you're ready, silently say: "I hope you are happy, healthy, and strong. I hope you feel peaceful and have fun today with your family and friends." Silently repeat these wishes or choose other wishes and put them into your own words.

8. Are there more people you'd like to send friendly wishes to? Picture them in your head and silently say: "I want you to be happy, strong, and healthy. I want you to feel peaceful and safe. I hope you have a great day." Repeat these wishes or choose other wishes you'd like to send to your friends and family and say them silently.

9. Now let's send friendly wishes to everyone on the planet. In your own words, silently say something like: "I hope everyone is happy, healthy, safe, and living in peace."

10. Now open your eyes, feel your body against the floor again, and sit up slowly. Reach your hands high up to the sky as you take a big breath in, and as you breathe out, lower your hands to your knees.

Regardless of age, it's common for meditators to find it hard to send themselves friendly wishes. It's also common for it to be difficult, if not impossible, for meditators of any age to send good wishes to someone who has treated them badly. Dr. Trudy Goodman, founder and guiding teacher of InsightLA, offers an innovative way to **Reframe** the next game—*Friendly Wishes for Difficult People*— for kids who have trouble with it. When children understand that sending friendly wishes is for their own benefit, rather than for the benefit of the difficult person, sending friendly wishes can be a simple yet liberating way for them to let go of painful feelings like helplessness, anger, or frustration. Recognizing that the difficult person would probably be less difficult if he or she felt happier and more confident is another way Goodman encourages children to **Reframe** the game. *Friendly Wishes for Difficult People* doesn't mean that kids need to change the way they feel about someone, nor that they should like someone whom they don't like. Equally important, it doesn't mean that they'll be better people if they spend time with someone whom they find it difficult to be with. The check-ins after kindness games are excellent opportunities to remind kids that it's smart to steer clear of challenging people, especially those who aren't kind or who make choices that aren't in their own best interests or the best interests of others.

It's important to keep a few things in mind when leading *Friendly Wishes for Difficult People*. As a practical matter, making a distinction between wishing someone well and liking someone is developmentally over the heads of young children. Encourage teens and older children to choose a person who "bugs" them or "gets on their nerves," not someone for whom their negative feelings are very strong. And remind kids that the people who bug and annoy them the most might also be the people whom they love the most. This can be a helpful discovery for children with siblings who get on their nerves.

friendly wishes for difficult people

We think of a person we find "difficult" and wish him or her well.

LIFE SKILLS Reframing, Caring, Connecting
TARGET AGES Older Children, Teens

LEADING THE GAME

1. Lie down or sit in a comfortable position and close your eyes.
2. Bring to mind an image of a person who is difficult for you to be around but whom you'd like to wish well.
3. Imagine that you feel happy. Imagine that you're smiling, laughing, and having fun. Don't worry if you don't feel happy right now. Just picture yourself laughing, hanging out with friends, or doing something that you love to do.
4. Then, in your own words, silently say something like: "I'd like to be happy. I want to feel healthy and strong. I hope to feel lots of love and to feel content and peaceful."
5. Now imagine that this feeling is warm and that it grows when you pay attention to it. Imagine the warm feeling starts near your heart, and as you silently say friendly wishes to yourself, the warm feeling reaches all the way to your fingers and toes, to your face, and to the top of your head. Imagine the warm feeling has a color, and you can see the color move from your heart, through your body, and out into the room.
6. Bring back the image of the person you find difficult whom you'd like to wish well. Remember, you don't need to change your feelings toward him or her. In your own words, silently say something like: "I want you to be healthy and content. I hope that you're safe and feel peaceful." Choose words and good wishes that you're comfortable saying and repeat them silently.
7. Now open your eyes. If you're lying down, sit up slowly. Take a breath and notice how you feel.

8. *Talking points: How did you feel before you sent friendly wishes? Was it easy or hard to do? How did you feel after sending a difficult person friendly wishes? Did your perspective on that person change?*

The room doesn't need to be quiet and people don't need to be still to send friendly wishes. Parents can send friendly wishes pushing a cart full of groceries through a busy supermarket, riding on a crowded train, or sitting behind the steering wheel in their car. Kids can send them waiting in the lunch line, riding the school bus, or sitting on the bleachers at a basketball game. And everyone can send friendly wishes as they walk along a busy sidewalk or sit in a loud theater waiting for a movie to begin.

In *Slow and Silent Walking* children anchored their attention to the sensations in their feet and legs while walking purposefully. In the next game, *Kindness with Every Step*, children walk silently, slowly, and purposefully too, but in this game every time they take a step they send a friendly wish. In both of these games children walk back and forth between a starting and an ending point. The instructions suggest that you use tape to mark where children start and stop walking and a bell to signal children when to begin. These tools aren't necessary, though. Children can walk between any starting and ending point, and you can cue them verbally.

kindness with every step

We walk slowly and purposefully. Every time we step, we silently send a friendly wish.

LIFE SKILLS Focusing, Caring   TARGET AGES All Ages

1. You'll begin at one line and slowly walk to the other line. Every time you step, you'll silently send a friendly wish. Keep your gaze downward to make it easier to concentrate.

2. When I ring the bell, start walking slowly toward the other line. Ring the bell.

3. Silently send yourself a friendly wish every time you step. "I want to be happy and strong. I hope I feel peaceful and content. May my old hurts fade away." You can use these wishes or choose wishes that you're more comfortable saying and repeat them silently.

4. When you get to the other line, slowly turn around and wait until you hear the bell—that will be your signal to start walking again. While you're waiting, keep sending friendly wishes to yourself. *Wait until everyone gets to the other line and then ring the bell.*

5. Let's walk back to the first line. This time, silently send a friendly wish to someone you love every time you step. In your own words, say something like: "I hope that you're happy. I want you to be safe, strong, and healthy." When you get to the other line, slowly turn around and wait until you hear the bell—that will be your signal to start walking again. While you're waiting, keep sending friendly wishes. *Ring the bell.*

6. Let's do it again. This time, every time you take a step silently send a friendly wish to someone you don't know well or someone you don't know at all. In your own words, say something like: "I hope you are content. I want you to have what you need." When you get to the other line, slowly turn around and wait until you hear the bell signaling you to start walking again. While you're waiting, keep sending friendly wishes. *When leading this game for young children, omit step number 7 and move directly to number 8.*

7. This time, when you walk from one line to the other, silently send

a friendly wish to a difficult person every time you step, if that's something you're comfortable doing. Choose someone who bugs you or who gets on your nerves, but not someone whom you have very strong negative feelings about. In your own words, say something like: "I hope you are happy. I hope you feel peaceful and content." Choose words and wishes that you're comfortable saying and repeat them silently. If you don't want to send friendly wishes to a difficult person, that's OK. Choose someone else instead or send friendly wishes to your pet or to yourself. When you get to the other line, slowly turn around and wait until you hear the bell. While you're waiting, keep sending friendly wishes.

8. Now, every time you take a step silently send a friendly wish to the planet, along with everyone and everything living on it. In your own words say something like: "I'd like everyone to be happy, healthy, and safe. I want all of us to be strong and live together peacefully. I hope that everyone has what he or she needs."

After some practice, you won't need to mark lines on the floor, and children will be ready to walk longer distances.

TIPS

1. Vary this game to emphasize the theme Appreciation (rather than Kindness) by playing *Thankful with Every Step*. Just follow the instructions for *Kindness with Every Step* but every time children take a step, silently have them say "thank you" to someone (or about something) they appreciate.

A growing body of research shows that classical loving-kindness practices have a beneficial long-term impact on adults, even in small doses. In *Psychology Today's* online magazine, Dr. Emma M. Seppälä from the Center for Compassion and Altruism Research and Education at Stanford University, and the author of *The Happiness Track*, posted a practical, easy-to-understand review of current research on the effect of kindness visualizations on adults. Studies have found that kindness visualizations improve (1) *emotional intelligence*, by activating empathy and emotional processing in the brain; (2) the *stress response*, by decreasing a chromosomal marker of aging known as telomere length; (3) *social connection*, by making us more helpful people, increasing compassion, increasing empathy, decreasing our biases toward others, and increasing our sense of social connection; (4) *self-love*, by curbing self-criticism; and (5) *well-being*, by increasing positive emotions, decreasing negative emotions, and increasing vagal tone. (Remember the vagus nerve from the section on **Quieting**? It's a complex cranial nerve that's sometimes referred to as the most important nerve in the body because it supports social engagement and mental well-being.)

The internal progression in kindness visualizations, in which children and teenagers wish themselves well first, before sending goodwill to other people and the community, tracks a sequence they've explored before. The sequential progression of **the ABCs** starts with self-awareness and the development of **attention** and **balance**, and then it moves to awareness of others and the development of **compassion**. Kids zoom in and take a look at what's happening inside them before zooming out and taking a look at the bigger picture of what's happening around them. *Friendly Wishes* folds this process of zooming in and zooming out into one introspective activity. Zooming in reminds children to be kind to themselves, and zooming out reminds them to be kind to other people and the planet.

— 9 —

OUT OF
OUR HEADS

In this chapter, children and teens will tune in to their bodies and minds using a meditation method known as a body scan. A *body scan* for adults can take between half an hour and forty-five minutes. However, if time is short or if the body scan is for kids, it can be done more quickly. In *Coming to Our Senses*, Jon Kabat-Zinn describes the method: "It involves systematically sweeping through the body with the mind, bringing an affectionate, openhearted, interested attention to its various regions. You can do a one in-breath one out-breath body scan, or a one-, two-, five-, ten-, or twenty-minute body scan. The level of precision and detail will of course vary depending on how quickly you move through the body." It makes sense that paying close attention to physical sensations helps children and teens get to know their bodies. Kids and parents are often surprised, though, by how much they learn about their feelings when they pay attention to what's happening in their bodies.

Like kindness visualizations, body scans and other sensory-based games sometimes bring up strong emotions that can be scary and feel overwhelming. Paying close attention to their bodies or to specific parts of their bodies can be especially difficult for kids who have suffered from trauma, illness, abuse, neglect, or a negative body image. Meditation teacher and psychotherapist Trudy Goodman suggests that children who have a history of trauma or who find body scans to be difficult practice them for just a short period of time. Even when longer body scans are unsettling, a few minutes of focusing on the sensations in their bodies can be helpful and soothing. In *Growing Up Mindful*, Dr. Christopher Willard suggests that children who find body scans to be difficult instead try grounding activities that focus on external anchors through the five senses.

Goodman offers two fun ways for kids to use external anchors to observe different parts of their bodies. The first is to send their bodies friendly wishes by silently saying phrases like *May my foot be warm and cozy in this slipper, may my legs be strong when I ride my bike, may I go to the beach this weekend and wiggle my toes in the sand, may my tummy be full.* Or they can thank their bodies by silently repeating *Thank you feet for standing, walking, running, skipping, and dancing, may you be happy, safe, and strong.* Other examples of grounding games that focus on external anchors are *Mira's Game* at the end of this chapter and, in earlier chapters, *Shake It Up, One Bite at a Time, Fading Tone, Slow and Silent Walking, Balloon Arms, Slowly, Slowly,* and *Rock-a-Bye.*

The games *Mind-Body Connection* and *Seeing Clearly* in chapter 2 helped children understand that what they think affects how they feel. Several of the relational games that come later in the book will also help kids become more aware of how their bodies and emotions are connected. Another lively, straightforward way for children and teens to notice a connection between what's happening in their minds and bodies in the moment is to play *Mind, Body, Go!* Children roll a ball back and forth as they quickly name a sensation and an emotion that they're feeling right now. It can be played with or without a ball in partners sitting across from one another, or with a group sitting in a circle.

mind, body, go!

We roll a ball back and forth as we quickly name a physical sensation and an emotion that we're feeling right now.

LIFE SKILLS Focusing, Seeing   TARGET AGES All Ages

LEADING THE GAME

1. We're going to roll this ball to one another, and when it's your turn, quickly name one thing that you're feeling in your mind and one thing that you're feeling in your body. Here's an example: "My body feels relaxed, and my mind feels happy."
2. I'll start: "My body feels stiff, and my mind feels a little nervous." *Roll the ball to your partner or to another child in the circle.*
3. Now you name something and roll the ball back. (For example, "My foot itches, and I feel silly.")
   Guide children in speeding up the pace as the play continues.

TIPS

1. Play *Mind, Body, Go!* without a ball while sitting around the kitchen table, or sitting in the car when you're stuck in traffic.

Body scans in MBSR, like the progressive muscle-relaxation exercises used in many gym and drama classes, start at the toes and move up to the head. My meditation teachers taught their students to scan through the body in the opposite direction, starting at the head and moving down to the toes. There's no consensus as to which direction is preferable or whether the direction that we choose matters very much. I use a head-to-toe progression because it steers my mind away from thinking and toward sensation. This helps me and many of the children and parents with whom I've shared mindfulness practices get out of our heads and into our bodies. In the next game, *Special Star*, children use their attention to scan their bodies by starting with their heads and ending with their toes.

special star

We imagine a special star in the night sky that helps us relax our bodies and quiet our minds.

LIFE SKILLS Focusing   TARGET AGES All Ages

LEADING THE GAME

1. Sit or lie down comfortably with your eyes closed. Breathe naturally, noticing how it feels to breathe in and out.

2. Imagine that there is a star in the sky just for you. It can look like anything at all—it can be any color, made out of any material, and it may change from moment to moment and day to day, just as everything changes. Sometimes large and sometimes small, sometimes bright and sometimes dim, your star is always there.

3. Let's feel the warmth of the star on different parts of our bodies.
   - As the starlight shines on your forehead, feel your forehead relax and imagine that all of the stress and strain of the day fade away.
   - Then imagine that the starlight shines on your shoulders…arms… hands…chest…belly and lower back…legs…ankles…and feet.
   - And finally, imagine your whole body relaxing in the warmth of the starlight.
   - Feeling relaxed, and with our whole bodies bathed in starlight, let's rest a little while longer.

4. When you're ready, sit up slowly and reach your hands to the sky. Take a deep breath in and lower your arms as you breathe out.

5. *Talking points: What happened in your mind and body during the body scan? Have you felt that way before, and if so, when?*

One of the greatest benefits of mindful attention is its flexibility. Mindfulness develops kids' capacity to shift attention between different types of experiences—from thoughts to emotions to sensations, for instance. In Mindfulness-Based Cognitive Therapy (MBCT), a clinical program that's based on MBSR and developed by Drs. Zindel Segal, Mark Williams, and Jon Teasdale, body scans demonstrate that attention can be moved from place to place. The next game gives children and teens an opportunity to do just that. It can be played with children seated, standing, or lying down.

butterfly body scan

With the help from an imaginary butterfly, we move our attention from one part of our body to another.

LIFE SKILLS Focusing   TARGET AGES All Ages

LEADING THE GAME

1. Sit or lie down comfortably with your eyes closed. Breathe naturally, noticing how it feels to breathe in and out.
2. Now picture a beautiful butterfly that's as light as a feather. It can be any color you like. Take a minute and focus on your butterfly.
3. Imagine your magic globe floating nearby. We're going to pretend that the butterfly rests on different parts of our body, and when it lands, that part of our body feels relaxed and pleasant.
4. Let's start with our foreheads. Imagine your forehead relaxes when the butterfly rests on it.
5. Imagine the butterfly floats off of your forehead and moves to one shoulder and rests. That shoulder relaxes.
   Continue with the image of the butterfly resting on different parts of the body.
6. Relax your whole body and rest, feeling the steady rhythm of your breathing.

7. When you're ready, take a deep breath in and reach your hands to the sky. Lower your arms as you breathe out.

In one of Annaka Harris's classes, children were invited to create their own mindfulness games, and a five-year-old girl named Mira came up with one that is remarkably insightful. Like *Butterfly Body Scan*, *Mira's Game* is a way for children to practice moving their attention deliberately from one type of sensation to another.

mira's game

We shift our attention—from seeing to feeling, to moving and back to seeing again—to help us notice all of the different things we can be aware of in every moment.

LIFE SKILLS Focusing   TARGET AGES Young Children, Older Children

LEADING THE GAME

1. Take a seat with your back straight and muscles relaxed, resting your hands gently on your knees. I'll place a stone on the floor in front of you to look at.
2. When I ring the bell pick up the stone, close your eyes, and **feel** the stone in your hands for a few breaths.
   Ring the bell.
3. The next time I ring the bell open your eyes and **look** at the stone for a few breaths.
   Ring the bell.
4. When I ring the bell again **place** the stone back on the floor and **look** at it for a few more breaths.
   Ring the bell again.

5. Let's try the whole series again. This time we'll run through it without talking. I'll just ring the bell for each step:
- Bell 1: Pick up the stone, close your eyes, and **feel** the stone in your hands—breathe.
- Bell 2: Open your eyes and **look** at the stone in your hands—breathe.
- Bell 3: **Place** the stone back on the floor in front of you and **look** at it on the floor—breathe.

TIPS

1. Play this game in pairs or, if playing with more than one child, in a circle. At the end of each round, ask children to place their stones in front of the child sitting to their left. That way, in the next round, everyone has a different stone to look at and feel.
2. To personalize the game, ask each child to bring a special rock, shell, leaf, or other object to use in *Mira's Game*.

Playing the games in the section on **Quieting**, kids learned that stress is not necessarily bad or good, that different people respond to stress differently, and that stress can be helpful when properly managed. After all, a little anxiety can motivate a teenager to excel on an exam or in a sporting event. The key to managing stress lies in children's noticing when their stress response has become so strong that it's starting to take over. Through sensory-based activities (like body scans) kids learn to recognize the body-based signals that let them know they're beginning to tip out of balance. The earlier kids recognize these signals, the more likely they'll be able to dampen an overly heightened stress response by holding back from mulling over the stressful experience, relaxing, and shifting their attention to a simple, neutral anchor until their minds and bodies quiet.

Part Four

Caring

An acrobat and his apprentice are asked to perform on a bamboo pole that stands in the middle of a town square. While getting ready, the acrobat tells his apprentice, "I'll climb the pole first. You come after me and stand on my shoulders. Once we're up there, you look after my balance, and I'll look after yours." Seems like a reasonable request, right? Not to the apprentice, who responds, "That won't work. You need to take care of your own balance, and I need to take care of mine. Otherwise we'll both fall and get hurt." As cheeky as she might sound, she's making a subtle and important point; the apprentice can only take care of the acrobat if she first takes care of herself. Flight attendants remind us of this every time we fly. Just as passengers on an airplane keep other people in mind by putting on their own oxygen masks first in an emergency, the apprentice keeps the acrobat in mind when she looks after her own balance. Like mindfulness, meditation, and other creative endeavors, some of the qualities of balance are mysterious and thus difficult, if not impossible, to describe. To know that we're in balance we have to feel balanced. As the apprentice told the acrobat, no one can find our balance for us—we have to find it ourselves.

Parents often put their family's needs above their own, even when setting aside their own needs comes at a cost. To borrow from Thich Nhat Hanh, "If we do not know how to take care of ourselves and to love ourselves, we cannot take care of the people we love." It's easy to forget that we're not much good to anyone when we're tired and rundown. Stress, strong emotions, exhaustion, plus other factors narrow our windows of tolerance and make us feel out of balance. When experiences that usually feel tolerable start to feel intolerable, our nervous systems are signaling us to recalibrate and take better care of ourselves. To do so requires healthy interpersonal boundaries. When the themes of mindfulness and meditation are misunderstood and improperly taught, they have the potential to undermine the development of the healthy boundaries that kids and parents need to successfully balance home, school, friendships, schedules, and work. Just telling someone to be nice, kind, thankful, generous, or balanced, or to take care of themselves, isn't very helpful, and it can be especially frustrating for kids who are looking for guidance on how best to respond to a thorny situation. Life is too complicated for generalizations like these. Kids and parents need concrete tools to help them recognize when other people's behavior is out of bounds and to take care of themselves.

When properly understood and taught, the themes and life skills explored through mindfulness and meditation nurture healthy boundaries by developing discernment, which is defined by the *Oxford English Dictionary* as "the ability to judge well." Discernment is one of the central themes of a wise and compassionate worldview. Through the exercise of discernment, kids and their parents learn to wisely prioritize other universal themes like kindness, appreciation, and acceptance over results—in their speech, in their actions, and in their relationships.

— 10 —

IS IT HELPFUL?

Kids have all kinds of habits. Some are physical (cracking knuckles, twirling hair), some are verbal (using certain words or phrases), and some are psychological (worrying, daydreaming, judging, overanalyzing). Habits run automatically, and because of the way brains are wired, repeating a habit reinforces the brain circuits associated with it, making it more difficult to overcome. In the section on **Focusing**, kids learned that when neurons fire together, they wire together—in other words, that the more they work a specific neural network, the more it changes, and the greater the effect. Imagine walking through a park and coming upon a large field of tall grass with a well-trod path cutting through the middle. What's the fastest and easiest way to get to the other side? Taking the existing path, of course, so that's what children are likely to do.

Brains are shaped by neural pathways much as walking paths shape fields. Both types of paths get better established through repeated use. Neural pathways are based in part on genetics, but they are also shaped by what children say, do, and think as well as children's life experiences. The more children and teens travel those old neural pathways—through their thoughts, speech, and actions—the more likely the activity in their brains will travel those pathways automatically. That's how certain ways of thinking, speaking, and acting become habitual. The stronger the habit, the stronger the neural pathways associated with it, and the stronger the effort and determination that will be required to break it. Here's an example. If kids check social media first thing in the morning, every morning, checking social media will soon become their default, automatic response to waking up. Even if they say, "You know, maybe I shouldn't do this every morning," their questioning will not be strong enough to overcome the urge to check. Motivation alone isn't enough. To break a habit requires motivation plus repeated action.

When it comes to the bundle of human qualities called "personal character," actions are the vehicles that drive its development, and awareness is the jumping-off point. First, children and teens identify the qualities they hope to embody, and next they develop those qualities through repeated actions that are consistent with their motivation. Here's where making and breaking habits can get tricky, though. Kids have habits that they know about and habits that they don't know about. Even when children hope to embody positive qualities, when they're not aware of negative ones, they can unwittingly reinforce them. To make changing the habits they don't know about even more difficult, the actions that reinforce those habits come easily because the neural pathways that lead in their direction are well established. That's why children and teenagers might not realize they're headed in the wrong direction until they're pretty far along a path. That's OK, though; at first their goal is simply to become aware of their habits and their motivation.

Mindful attention is a handy tool to bring habits into awareness in a way that's similar to how utility software programs find glitches on a computer. Think of the brain as a computer hard drive where information about a child's inner and outer world is stored automatically. Unnecessary data on a hard drive can cause a glitch that slows the computer down. Utility programs take care of this problem by periodically searching for glitches and fixing them. Just as software programs search for glitches, kids can direct mindful attention to search for habits of their minds and bodies. Unlike software programs, though, mindful attention can't tell a wise habit from a glitch, nor can it break a bad habit on its own.

To make a wise habit or break an unwise one, kids need discernment. To understand what the word *discernment* means in this context, it's helpful to understand a little bit about karma, a Sanskrit word with roots in Buddhism and Hinduism that means "cause and effect." In popular culture the word *karma* is often used incorrectly to mean "preordained," yet a more accurate definition of its meaning is that "actions have consequences." Actions include what children do, say, and think. All actions, even small ones, have ramifications. Kids discern whether or not an action is wise by considering their motivation together with cause and effect. Discernment, motivation, and cause and effect are three of the themes woven through a wise and compassionate worldview that we're exploring in this book.

The next game offers children and teens a sequence of questions to help them discern whether a habit, a response to a tricky situation, or frankly anything they might say or do is wise. When working with families, I substitute the word *helpful* for the word *wise* because its definition is clear and in most children's vocabularies by a young age. I landed on the word when I heard Gay MacDonald, who was the director of UCLA's early childcare centers at the time, ask a four-year-old who was acting up on the playground whether what she was doing was helpful. That brief encounter was like a master class in teaching discernment to young children. Because of its neutrality and lack of emotional charge, the word *helpful* is indeed helpful when one is sharing mindfulness with older children, teens, and parents, too. When introducing the series of questions in the game *Is It Helpful?* I'm not suggesting that kids stop, reflect, and run through a series of questions every time they're about to do or say something, only when they find themselves in a complex situation in which choosing an appropriate response requires some thought.

is it helpful?

When we're not sure if something we're about to do or say is thoughtful and kind, we ask ourselves a series of questions.

LIFE SKILLS Reframing, Caring, Connecting   TARGET AGES All Ages

LEADING THE DISCUSSION

1. Can you give an example of a complicated situation when it was hard for you to decide how to respond?
   After children offer examples, choose one of them.
2. What do you think would be the best thing to do or say in this situation?
   After children offer ideas, choose one of them.
3. Let's ask three questions to see if this response is a wise choice: "Is it helpful to me? Is it helpful to other people? Is it helpful to the planet?"

Asking children and teens to check in and see if a response is helpful to them before considering whether it's helpful to others isn't an implied message for kids to prioritize their own interests over their friends' or the community's. I encourage children and teens to check in with themselves first because it's difficult, if not impossible, to see other people and their experiences clearly unless kids are self-aware. They've already considered the sequence in which the **ABCs—attention, balance,** and **compassion**—are taught in classical meditation training and learned why meditators develop self-awareness first, before developing awareness of other people and the world around them. Children and teens saw a parallel internal progression in *Friendly Wishes*, when they sent friendly wishes to themselves before sending them to others. The internal progression of the questions in *Is It Helpful?* is another example in which mindfulness starts with zooming in, so kids can reflect on how an action would affect them, before zooming out, so they can reflect on how it would affect other people and the planet.

Whether a response is helpful is not always clear-cut, and as a practical matter, there are situations when children and teens must choose between competing but equally important priorities. At times like these, the Dalai Lama offers the following advice in *Beyond Religion*: "Matters of ethics are often not black and white. After checking to be sure that we are motivated by concern for the welfare of humanity, we must weigh the pros and the cons of the various paths open to us and then let ourselves be guided by a natural sense of responsibility. This, essentially, is what it means to be wise." It's no surprise that kids' answers to the questions "Is it helpful to me, other people, and the planet?" often conflict. Differences of opinion offer a welcome opportunity to revisit *Pinky Pointing*, the game in which a group of children simultaneously answer a question with hand gestures. *Pinky Pointing* illustrates that people's opinions differ in a playful and dramatic way. It has the added benefit of not inadvertently putting a child on the spot by singling her out to answer a potentially loaded question in front of her friends. When kids' answers conflict, I ask a fourth question: "What matters most in this situation?"

Behavioral restraint is another of the themes that support a wise and compassionate worldview. It is an innate quality that's made stronger through mindfulness and meditation. Defined by the Dalai Lama in *Beyond Religion* as "deliberately refraining from doing actual or potential harm to others," restraint gives children an opportunity to compose themselves when they're upset, overly excited, or having a hard time controlling what they say or do. In *Conscious Discipline*, Dr. Becky Bailey equates composure with "self-control in action" and points out that "composure is a choice we can make, regardless of how crazy the outside world appears to be." Children and teens' ability to exercise behavioral restraint is, at least in part, dependent on their age and level of maturation. The younger the children, the more difficulty they generally have holding back or waiting for anything—from a turn to getting something they want to saying something. More mature children generally find restraint to be easier. Regardless of age, the more excited or worked up kids become, the tougher it is for them to inhibit a response. Children's ability to think before speaking or acting also suffers when they are tired or stressed. The same holds true for adults.

In my experience, the development of behavioral restraint has been a game-changing aspect of meditation and mindfulness, especially for young children, and it can happen pretty early in the process. Even children as young as four can quickly learn that if they stop to feel their breathing they'll be more focused and calm when they start something new.

i stop and feel my breathing

We sing a song to learn that if we want to feel calmer and more focused, we can stop and feel our breathing.

LIFE SKILLS Focusing, Quieting   TARGET AGES Young Children

LEADING THE GAME

1. *Talking points: What do you feel like when you're excited? It can be hard to control our voices and bodies when we're excited, right? Sometimes when I feel overly excited and need help controlling my voice or my body, I stop and feel my breathing.*
2. I'm going to sing a song called "I Stop and Feel My Breathing." It goes like this:

   I stop (palms facing out like a stop sign)
   And feel my breathing (hands on belly)
   Peaceful and calm, I'm ready to . . . (eat, read, learn)

   An audio file of this song is posted on
   www.susankaisergreenland.com/resources/downloads.
3. Let's sing it together.
4. *Talking points: How do you feel when you stop and notice your breathing? How might this help you in everyday life?*

TIPS

1. The last phrase of the song depends on what children are planning to do next. For example, if they are going to read a book, the last phrase would be "Peaceful and calm, I'm ready to read."

I Stop and Feel My Breathing is a playful way to give children an opportunity to practice behavioral restraint. I also encourage them to use mindful prompts.

mindful prompts

We use nonverbal prompts to help compose ourselves and concentrate.

LIFE SKILLS Focusing, Seeing
TARGET AGES Young Children, Older Children

EXAMPLES OF PROMPTS

1. **Quieting Signals**

   If a child is speaking out of turn, rather than asking her to stop, try using a nonverbal approach by making eye contact, smiling, and putting your finger to your lips, bringing your hand to your ear, or pointing in the direction where her attention should be focused.

2. **Hands Up**

   Raise your hand so that everyone who can see you knows to do the same. When your hand is up, it means there's no talking, and eyes and ears are on you. A variation on the hands-up signal is to use a verbal cue asking for a nonverbal gesture in response. If you're sharing mindfulness with a group of children and they can't all see you, raise your hand as you say: "If you hear my voice, raise your hand."

3. **Clap and Repeat**

   Children stop what they are doing and listen when you clap out a sequence and then they repeat it back. Children soon learn to recognize the clapping sequence as a nonverbal cue to listen and pay attention. Clap and repeat has the added benefit of training attention.

4. **Slow Motion**

By deliberately slowing down and being more conscious of your movements, you cue children to do the same. Slow motion helps children develop attention and self-control as they become aware of what's happening within and around them. Saying "Move slowly like a sloth" is a fun verbal cue that prompts children who are familiar with the book *"Slowly, Slowly, Slowly," Said the Sloth* by Eric Carle to move slowly and deliberately.

5. **Zip-Up**

Once children are familiar with the game *Zip-Up*, it can be used as a mindful prompt. Cue *Zip-Up* nonverbally by placing one hand in front of your belly button and the other hand at your lower back. Wait until children mimic you. Then mime zipping up by moving your hands up your spine and chest, passing your chin and head, and ending with your hands in the air; children will follow. Wait until all the children have their hands in the air, then give a silent cheer.

6. **Balloon Arms**

Balloon Arms can also be used as a mindful prompt strategy. Cue *Balloon Arms* nonverbally by resting the palms of both hands on the top of your head, with the tips of your fingers touching. Children will mimic you by putting their hands on their heads, too. Wait until everyone is ready before raising your arms to mime a balloon inflating (keeping your fingers together) and lowering your arms to mime a balloon deflating.

Mindful prompts interrupt mindless, automatic behavior and create some space for kids to stop and notice how they feel in that moment. The prompts above are more oriented toward children, but there are mindful prompts lurking everywhere for preteens, teens, and parents, too. Here are a few simple ones:

• When a phone rings, buzzes, or dings, see if there's any tension in your body. If there is, soften the muscles around it.

• Curb an impulse to automatically check social media and move your attention to an experience in the moment instead (the sounds in the room, the sensation of breathing, the horizon, a leaf or flower on a nearby plant, a peaceful image in your head).
• Before eating a snack, think of the many people who were part of the chain of events that led to its being in your hand. Thank them either silently or out loud.
• While standing in line, send friendly wishes to the other people waiting with you.

As older children and teens come to understand their habits, they begin to see when they have automatic, knee-jerk reactions to pleasant, unpleasant, and neutral experiences. In the next game, older children and teens notice these three categories of life experiences and learn to hold back from reacting to them reflexively. To prepare, place one or two ice cubes in a cup for each person and set out paper towels.

melting ice

We hold a cube of ice until it melts so we can notice the difference between a feeling and a reaction.

LIFE SKILLS Focusing, Seeing   TARGET AGES Older Children, Teens

LEADING THE GAME
1. *Talking points: Before you pick up the ice, notice how you feel. What thoughts are you having? What are you feeling in your body?*
2. Now we're going to pick up a piece of ice and hold it until it melts. It might feel uncomfortable to hold the ice, but it's safe and won't hurt you. Let's hold the ice over the paper towel, so we don't get the floor wet.

3. If the ice feels uncomfortable, take a few deep breaths and relax your hand and arm. If holding the ice is too hard, don't worry—put it down for a moment, then pick it back up and try again.

4. Without talking, notice how the ice feels in your hand as it melts. Do you like how it feels? Do you not like it? Do you want to drop it? *Wait about thirty to sixty seconds before moving to the next step.*

5. Notice how your hand feels now. Are the feelings in your hand changing? What about your thoughts? *Ask children to squeeze the ice, shift the ice to different parts of their hands, or move the ice to their other hand, noticing what happens with each change.*

6. *Talking points: Describe how the feelings in your hand changed the longer you held the ice. Did you want to drop the ice? Describe how your thoughts and emotions changed while you held the ice.*

Next, children use a colorful Awareness Meter to explore how they react to pleasant, unpleasant, and neutral experiences. As a general rule, kids are attracted to pleasant experiences and want to hold onto them. They want to get rid of unpleasant experiences, and they're often bored by neutral experiences and feel restless. Even though these reactions to pleasant, unpleasant, and neutral experiences are different from one another, they have the same effect. Regardless of whether kids are chasing after pleasant experiences or trying to get rid of unpleasant or boring ones, they miss out on what's happening in the moment. This needn't discourage them, though. As Pema Chödrön explains in *Awakening Loving-Kindness,* "One of the main discoveries of meditation is seeing how we continually run away from the present moment, how we avoid being here just as we are. That's not considered to be a problem; the point is to see it." Awareness may be the point of meditation, but it isn't enough to change habitual patterns of thought or behavior. Awareness can inspire us to do the work that's necessary to change unhelpful habits and make helpful ones, however, by changing the way we perceive them. The next two games use visual aids called Awareness Meters to demonstrate this important point to children.

Like *Pinky Pointing*, a game that children learned in chapter 3, Awareness Meters make it possible for more than one person to answer the same question at the same time. The meters are deliberately neutral in design to help children become aware of their thoughts, emotions, and sensations without an overlay of judgments. For the next game you'll need the two meters that are printed at the end of this book—one for you and one for your child. Children can personalize their meters by coloring the triangles with markers or crayons.

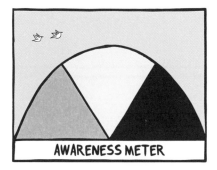

awareness meter

We use an Awareness Meter to help us notice how we're feeling and communicate it to others.

LIFE SKILLS Focusing, Seeing   TARGET AGES All Ages

LEADING THE GAME

1. I'm going to ask a question and both of us will answer at the same time by pointing to a color on our Awareness Meter.

   Keep one meter and hand a second meter to the child.

2. When I say "Go" point to the lightest color if you're paying attention to what's happening here in the room and point to the darkest color if you're thinking about something or someplace else. Let's both keep our fingers on the color so you can see my response and I can see yours. Remember, the point of this game is to notice what's happening in our minds and bodies in the moment; there aren't any right or wrong answers. 1-2-3-GO!

Point to a color on the meter, and children will do the same.

3. That's interesting. Now I have another question. When I asked you what you were paying attention to in the last round, was your mind in the past, the present, or the future? If you were thinking about the past point to the darkest triangle, if you were thinking about the future point to the lightest triangle, and if you were thinking about the present point to the triangle in the middle. 1-2-3-GO!

4. Remember to keep your finger on the color so I can see your response.

Talking points: How often does your mind wander? Can you give an example of when being distracted is not helpful? Can you give an example of when being distracted is helpful? Is daydreaming helpful, unhelpful, or does it depend on the situation?

TIPS

1. If you don't have Awareness Meters, children can answer questions with *Pinky Pointing*. Teenagers might be more receptive to answering questions with a thumbs-up, thumbs-down, or thumbs sideways than with their pinkies.

2. There are more examples of questions that can be asked and answered with an Awareness Meter in the instructions for *Pinky Pointing*.

Awareness Meter and *Pinky Pointing* are useful tools when facilitating a discussion about how to best respond in a challenging situation.

To lay the groundwork for these potentially loaded conversations, start by exploring common automatic reactions to experiences that are not emotionally charged, like in the next game, where children notice how they react to different sounds. To prepare, collect musical instruments and place them out of view of the children.

"what did i hear?" with awareness meters

We listen to the sounds around us and notice how they make us feel.

LIFE SKILLS Focusing, Seeing   TARGET AGES All Ages

LEADING THE GAME

1. Sit with your back straight and your body relaxed, resting your hands gently on your knees. Close your eyes if that's comfortable for you. Notice what it feels like to breathe in and out right now.
2. I'm going to make some sounds with different instruments. You don't have to make any extra effort to hear them. Just relax and listen. *Make different sounds using instruments or interesting objects—a shaker, a string instrument, tapping rocks together, shaking coins, for example.*
3. Listen closely and see if you can guess what's making the sounds. Just relax and wait for the sounds to appear like little surprises. Try to remember what you heard, because I want to hear your guesses at the end. *Continue making sounds for about a minute.*
4. *Talking points: Were you able to guess what was making any of the sounds? Were you surprised by what you heard? What was it like to hear different sounds with your eyes closed? Hand an Awareness Meter to each child and keep one for yourself.*

5. I'm going to make some sounds again but this time I want you to notice how you feel about the different sounds. If a sound is pleasant point to the darkest triangle on the meter and if it's unpleasant point to the lightest triangle. If you don't feel one way or the other about a sound, point to the center triangle. Keep your finger on the color so we can see how everyone is feeling.

   Make sounds using the same instruments or objects as before. Leave enough time between each sound for children to react by pointing to a triangle on their Awareness Meter.

6. *Talking points: Did you want pleasant sounds to last? Did you want unpleasant sounds to stop? Did your body react to the sounds? Did your body react the same way to every sound?*

Mindful Prompts, Melting Ice, Awareness Meters, What Did I Hear? and *Pinky Pointing* are games that strengthen **Focusing** and **Seeing**. As these life skills grow stronger, kids begin to trust that they'll be able to compose themselves when they feel overly excited and upset. As a result, they'll be more likely to have the confidence to try new things, experiment with new ideas, and be creative.

— 11 —

FLOODLIGHT
OF ATTENTION

Like the mom I described in the chapter on mindful breathing who stopped meditating because she was overwhelmed by strong feelings, the dad who stopped meditating because he got lost in thought or zoned out, and me when I was learning to meditate, many kids are afraid they'll fall apart if they give up trying to manage the thoughts and emotions that are bouncing around in their heads. What none of us were able to recognize at first was that we were chasing, overanalyzing, avoiding, and overidentifying with our thoughts, beliefs, and feelings. The activity in our minds wasn't a problem, but how we reacted to it became one. In *Turning Confusion into Clarity*, Yongey Mingyur Rinpoche wrote that his father taught him about meditation by comparing the behavior of a bad shepherd with that of a good shepherd: "A bad shepherd has a narrow view. He might chase after one sheep that strays to the left but miss the one moving to the right, so he ends up running in circles like a dog chasing its tail." The master meditation teacher told his inquiring young son, "When we meditate we don't try to control all our thoughts and feelings. We just rest naturally, like the good shepherd, watchful and attentive."

In the last chapter, children learned that people's natural tendency to pursue pleasant thoughts and avoid unpleasant ones makes perfect sense by playing *Melting Ice* and games using an *Awareness Meter*. They also learned that if they're oblivious to what they're doing, they can get stuck chasing or running away from their thoughts and feelings. That's one of the reasons why *awareness* is so important. When kids realize that they're stuck, they have an opportunity to step back and reflect on what trapped them. Remember the story from chapter 4 about the monkey who wouldn't let go of a banana? Just as the monkey could have freed himself from the hunter's trap had he been willing to leave the banana alone, older kids and teens can wiggle out of their psychological traps by relaxing and letting their thoughts alone. Finger traps (sometimes known as Chinese or Mexican finger puzzles or handcuffs) are a useful visual and experiential metaphor for how to get free. To prepare, give each child a finger trap and keep one for yourself.

finger trap

When we pull on finger traps, our fingers get stuck; but when we relax and stop pulling, our fingers are set free.

LIFE SKILLS Focusing, Seeing   TARGET AGES Older Children, Teens

LEADING THE GAME

1. Place your pinky fingers in the two ends of the cylinder.
2. Pull your fingers away from each other, like this, and try to pull your fingers out of the trap.
   The cylinders will narrow, and children's fingers will get trapped.
3. Now stop pulling, relax, and breathe. Move your fingers back toward each other.

4. *Talking points: What's the best way to release your fingers from the trap? How is getting your fingers stuck in the trap similar to getting caught up in thoughts, emotions, and stress?*

The games in this chapter call upon the floodlight of attention to help older kids understand their minds. The floodlight of attention is a wide, receptive beam that lights up a broad field of changing experience. Games that use the floodlight are called awareness games; in them, kids exercise contemplative restraint, one of the themes we're exploring in this book, by noticing what shows up in their inner and outer worlds (thoughts, feelings, sensations, sounds, temperatures) without reacting to it. Chögyam Trungpa Rinpoche describes the benefits of contemplative restraint in *Mindfulness in Action*: "This approach is not cutting off the thought process altogether, but is loosening it up. Thoughts become transparent and loose, so that they can pass through or float around in our minds more easily. Thoughts are often very heavy and sticky, and they hang around, demanding that we pay attention to them. But with this approach, the thought process becomes relaxed and fluid, fundamentally transparent. In this way, we learn to *relate* to our thought process, rather than trying to attain a state without thoughts altogether." When leading awareness games, it's important for parents to remember that young children aren't yet developmentally ready to hold back from reacting to their thoughts, emotions, and sensations. When I asked Mark Greenberg, Founding Director of the Prevention Research Center for the Promotion of Human Health at Penn State, at what age this metacognitive skill first develops, he answered that it

depends on the child but is unlikely to develop before the fourth grade. Awareness games can be easily modified to become anchor games that are appropriate for younger children, though, and I've included suggestions for how to adapt them.

It's also important that parents keep in mind that the way kids relate to distractions when they play awareness games that use the floodlight of attention is different from how they relate to distractions when they play anchor games that use the spotlight of attention. In anchor games, anything that pulls children's attention away from their anchor is a distraction. In awareness games, nothing is a distraction. When older children and teens stop chasing, over-analyzing, avoiding, and overidentifying with the activity in their minds, they're able to relate to it differently. As a result, the grip of troublesome beliefs, thoughts, and emotions starts to loosen and ease. Then kids are able to see what is happening within and around them with more clarity and equanimity. I use a bobblehead doll to demonstrate this "heady" concept.

bobblehead

We shake a bobblehead doll to help us understand how to leave thoughts and emotions alone, rather than reacting to them.

LIFE SKILLS Quieting   TARGET AGES Older Children, Teens

LEADING THE DEMONSTRATION
1. I sometimes feel like a bobblehead doll. When I'm excited, upset, or angry, my mind can start racing around in my head so fast that I feel like this.
   Shake the bobblehead and keep shaking it throughout the demonstration.
2. Have you ever felt like a bobblehead doll?

If the children don't offer examples, give a few of your own: "The time I was caught in traffic and worried that I'd be late for class. The time I looked all through the house for the book I was reading but never found it."

3. It's distracting when we feel like bobblehead dolls. The thoughts, emotions, and beliefs that are bouncing around in our heads feel like they need our attention. But if we try to pay attention to all of them, it's easy to get lost, and it's hard to think clearly.
Shake the bobblehead again.

4. What should we do?

5. *Talking points: Should we try to get rid of our thoughts? How? What would happen if we did nothing at all? What if we left our thoughts alone and didn't react to them?*
Set the bobblehead doll down on a solid surface; the movement of the head will slow and eventually stop.

6. Our thoughts and feelings don't go away entirely, nor do we want them to. But when we leave them alone, they eventually settle, and we can think clearly again.

7. *Talking points: What would happen if we started to mull over our thoughts again?*
Shake the bobblehead.

8. If we're in a difficult situation, it makes sense that our minds will get busy again, even after we've been able to quiet them. When that happens, if we relax and notice what's happening without reacting to it, our minds tend to settle down naturally.

To change the way they relate to their thoughts, feelings, and beliefs, children must first become familiar with them, and that requires concentration. That's why visualizations and anchor games that develop concentration (the spotlight of attention) are taught before the awareness games in this chapter that develop the floodlight of attention. Remember, it's a misunderstanding to consider the spotlight and floodlight as separate ways of paying attention, even though it's helpful to present them that way. To use a college metaphor coined by the American Lama Surya Das, awareness games are "like majoring in panoramic attention [the floodlight] and minoring in concentration [the spotlight]."

There's no better way for older children and teens to practice this relaxing, spacious, floodlight-like way of paying attention than by *Stargazing*. To prepare, find a comfortable spot from which to gaze at the sky and set up chairs or a blanket. Young children like gazing at the sky, too. The instructions below explain how to adapt this game so that it's appropriate for them as well.

stargazing

We relax and gaze at the sky to explore what's happening in the moment.

LIFE SKILLS Focusing, Caring   TARGET AGES Older Children, Teens (with a modification for Young Children)

LEADING THE GAME

1. Sit or lie down comfortably and settle into the natural rhythm of your breathing.
2. Look toward the horizon and lightly rest your gaze there. Keep your eyes soft, not focusing on any particular object.
3. Notice any changes that you see in the sky, moon, or stars.
4. When thoughts or feelings bubble up, you can just let them be. If you don't analyze or think about your thoughts and emotions, they tend to come, stay for a while, and then fade away on their own.

   When leading young children, replace step number 4 with this: "If you notice you're distracted and thinking about something else, that's OK—just feel your breathing for a few breaths and then go back to gazing at the sky."

5. *Talking points: What did you see? Were you surprised by what you saw? Did the sky stay the same? Did it change? Can you describe how you felt? How do you feel now?*

TIPS

1. Start by practicing *Stargazing* for a short time and build to longer periods.
2. In the daytime try *Cloudgazing*. Grab a beach chair or towel and find a shady spot outside. Encourage children to notice the leaves blowing in the wind, drifting clouds, and other changes in their environment.
3. *Stargazing* and *Cloudgazing* are great ways for children (and adults) to rest and take care of themselves when life is hectic and they feel stressed.

Stargazing is not about spacing out. It's about teaching older kids to let whatever bubbles up in their minds rise and fall naturally.

It's fine for stargazers to let their minds roam freely, provided that they're noticing what's happening in their heads. Even the most accomplished of meditators get lost in thought, though. To come back everyone, regardless of age, returns their gaze to the horizon.

This open, receptive method of meditation requires strong concentration, and many new meditators, young and old alike, find it to be difficult. Another, more structured way to work with thoughts is to label them "thinking," as older children and teens do in the next game.

resting and noticing

While relaxing and paying attention to the sensation of breathing, we note when thoughts and emotions distract us by silently saying the word "thinking."

LIFE SKILLS Focusing, Caring   TARGET AGES Older Children, Teens

LEADING THE GAME

1. Sit with your back straight and your body relaxed, resting your hands gently on your knees. Close your eyes if that's comfortable for you.
2. Let's find our breathing anchor again, just like we did in the *Mindful Breathing* game. Take a moment to see where you feel your breathing the most—near your nose, your chest, or your belly.
3. When you breathe out, see if you can lightly rest your attention on your exhale and stay with it all the way to the end. Let's do this for a few breaths.
4. Now, don't pay any special attention to your breathing. Just rest.
5. When thoughts and emotions bubble up, try not to think about them too much. The next time you notice a thought or emotion, just say the word "thinking" silently to yourself, and then rest while feeling the natural rhythm of your breathing.
6. The next time you silently say the word "thinking" notice your tone of voice.
   Continue guiding this meditation as long as children seem comfortable and engaged.

TIPS

1. The words "gently" and "lightly" are used in these instructions to prompt children to relax and take it easy on themselves.
2. These instructions encourage kids to rest their attention on the out-breath and stay with it all the way to the end. This steadies their attention and many kids find it to be relaxing and calming.

The last instruction in *Resting and Noticing* (step number 6) introduces a simple, straightforward way for older children and teens to practice self-awareness and self-compassion by noticing the tone of voice they use when they speak to themselves. When an inner heckler whispers insults in a child's ears, the difficult emotions that come in their wake feel real and can be overwhelming. Kids find freedom in knowing that their negative self-judgment isn't real while practicing compassion toward the part of them that believes it is. For older kids and teens, noticing the tone of voice they use when they speak to themselves, and considering whether it is the tone of a helpful friend or an unhelpful heckler, creates an opportunity to practice self-compassion. Silently saying the word *thinking* and noticing their inner tone of voice can be helpful to older kids when *Stargazing*, too.

Resting and Noticing and *Stargazing* facilitate rest and relaxation. Rest and relaxation are pretty great on their own, but they also offer many more benefits. When children and teens are relaxed and rested, they're able to investigate what's happening within and around them with a clear head and more ease. One of the first things they'll notice is that everything changes. Gazing at the sky, they'll observe that the quality of light and colors change; resting and noticing, they'll feel their breathing slow and deepen; listening mindfully, they'll hear sounds rise and fall; when they meditate, they'll watch their thoughts and feelings come and go. These observations are opportunities to talk with kids about how everything is in flux and always changing. When viewed in this way, the theme everything changes becomes a comfort, and it can be especially reassuring when life feels unfair. Tomorrow, things will be different, and whatever rough patch children might be going through now will eventually change.

Part Five

Connecting

On a gorgeous autumn day, while working in his garden, Lion finds a tiny bird with a broken wing. A flock of birds flies overhead, and as Lion bandages Bird's broken wing, the unlikely pair watch Bird's tribe head south. She has been left behind. They spend the winter in Lion's welcoming hut, reading and eating together and enjoying every day. Winter turns to spring, and Bird's flock returns. She gestures to Lion that she has to go, and Lion answers, "I know." We turn the page of the storybook we're reading to find a heartbreaking illustration of the first insight of mindfulness. Written beneath a melancholy drawing of Lion walking home alone are the words "Sometimes life is like that." Lion tends his garden, reads his books, and grows accustomed to living alone again. To his surprise and delight, when autumn returns, so does Bird, and they spend another cozy winter together. This story, *The Lion and the Bird* by Marianne Dubuc, is a stunning example of compassion in action.

Compassion prioritizes verbs over nouns and is tested in actions more than mind-sets. Most of the games in the first four sections of this book are introspective practices designed to help children cultivate wisdom and compassion by becoming aware of what's happening within and around them. The next set of games brings those qualities into children's actions and relationships purposefully. Compassion is not a solo, linear path but a dynamic one that is deeply rewarding, even though it sometimes requires sacrifice. Compassion comes relatively easily when kids feel it, but the true test is when they don't feel it and act compassionately anyway. The themes I selected for this book draw from traditions that are rich with meaning, but if I was pressed to choose just one lesson to pass on as the legacy of my work with children and families, this would be it: Let go of achievement and focus more on the goodness of what you're doing than on the result. Then, let the music play.

—— 12 ——

TO BE,
NOT TO SEEM

I catch sight of the Latin phrase *esse quam videri* while putting some mail that has been mistakenly delivered to our house in my grown daughter's old bedroom. It is written on a lime-green Post-it note that she stuck to the edge of her bookshelf several years ago. I grab a dictionary and look it up: "To be, rather than to seem." Later, I send her a text message asking for advice on a delicate matter. She texts back, "You do You," three single-syllable words that have a specific meaning to her but not to me. I search for "You do You" on the *Urban Dictionary* website: "The act of doing the things that you normally do. Nothing more, nothing less." Along with countless other classics students and rap music fans, my daughter walks the talk of empathy, attunement, and compassion, three universal themes that are crucial building blocks to a wise and compassionate worldview.

Even though they are often used interchangeably, each of these themes has a separate and distinctive meaning. *Empathy* is the capacity to understand what something looks and feels like from another person's point of view, while *attunement* describes the experience of feeling seen and understood. Seeing another person's perspective, understanding how they feel, and responding with wisdom and kindness is *compassion*. The differences between these themes might seem minor, but in the context of a living, breathing relationship they are meaningful. By way of example, children can empathize with someone (understand the other person's thoughts and feelings), but if they don't connect with that person, there's neither attunement (the other person doesn't feel seen and understood) nor compassion (they didn't respond to the other person wisely and with kindness). Kids can connect so deeply with someone who's suffering that they suffer too (they feel empathy and are attuned to the other person's experience), yet if they become so enmeshed in the other person's feelings that they're unable to see and respond to what's happening objectively, they're not able to respond with compassion. When my daughter answered my text, she was letting me know that she saw and understood what I was grappling with (she empathized), I felt seen and understood (we were attuned), and her encouragement to be myself was compassionate.

Understanding and sharing the feelings of another is a prerequisite to attunement and compassion; thus, empathy is the gateway to both. In *Conscious Discipline*, Becky Bailey explains that children's capacity to empathize emerges early in childhood and develops progressively through the teenage years. Before the age of six, children recognize that a friend is upset, but their expressions of comfort and sympathy might not be very helpful because they still view the world almost entirely through their own perspectives. Between six and nine, children's capacity to empathize with friends and family members becomes more reciprocal, even though it remains rather narrow and focused on specific situations that they can relate to. Later, in preadolescence, children begin to generalize and empathize with people living in different times, places, and cultures.

Older children and teens demonstrate *interpersonal attunement* when they tune in to another person's inner world with an open mind and the other person feels seen and understood. The term *attunement* is more often used to refer to how a parent responds to a child, however, than to how a child responds to a parent or friend. It is often paired with the term *attachment* to describe the emotional relationship between parent and child. An attached, attuned relationship creates a deep and enduring emotional bond that connects children with their parents over time and space. A secure attachment to a parent or other caregiver offers children the psychological safety of a home base from which they can venture out with confidence into a community that's larger than their nuclear families. How children view the world as adults, and how they steer their way through it, depends on many factors, including genetics, temperament, and IQ. One major predictor of how children will fare as adults is their early life experience. To parents this can feel like an enormous responsibility, even when they intellectually understand that there's no such thing as a perfect parent and that the ideal parent is just good enough.

Young children grow stronger and more autonomous when they respond to their parents' small failures appropriately and are able to roll with it when parents are cranky, late, or forgetful. Pediatrician and child analyst Dr. D. W. Winnicott, who coined the phrase "good-enough mother," explains that the good-enough mother "starts off with an almost complete adaptation to her infant's needs, and as time proceeds she adapts less and less completely, gradually, according to the infant's growing ability to deal with her failure. Her failure to adapt to every need of the child helps them adapt to external realities." Even the best-intentioned and most enlightened parent can't be perfectly in tune with his or her child all of the time. Luckily, perfection isn't necessary—thus the term *good enough*. Mistakes are not just OK, they're to be expected; what's important is that parents and children repair their mistakes by talking them through.

Dr. Mark Epstein, author of several books on meditation and psychotherapy, draws a connection between good-enough parenting and good-enough meditation in *The Trauma of Everyday Life*: "The steady application of the meditative posture, like the steadiness of an attuned parent, allows something inherent in the mind's potential to emerge, and it emerges naturally if left alone properly in a *good enough* way." The meditative posture that Epstein is referring to is an example of *internal attunement* (as opposed to interpersonal attunement). As with the spotlight of attention and the floodlight of attention, it would be a misunderstanding to consider internal and interpersonal attunement as entirely separate from one another, even though it's helpful to present them that way. Just as the floodlight of attention includes the spotlight, interpersonal attunement includes internal attunement; when parents are fully present with their children, they're attuned not only to their child's internal experiences but also to their own. Interpersonal and internal attunement happen all the time, both inside and outside of family relationships. When team members play together in a basketball game, they are attuned to one another and to themselves, as are actors when they're improvising a comedy sketch.

Describing mindfulness as "paying attention with kindness to me, other people, and the world" allows young children to practice differentiating between self and other even when they're in a developmental window that's described as egocentric. The next two games, *Your Own Bubble* and *Pass the Cup*, also help young children differentiate between self and other in a developmentally appropriate way.

your own bubble

We imagine a bubble around us so we can become aware of where our bodies are in relation to other people and things.

LIFE SKILLS Focusing, Caring, Connecting
TARGET AGES Young Children

1. *Talking points: Can you describe a bubble for me?*
2. I'm going to make an imaginary bubble around my body.
   Mark your bubble by drawing an imaginary circle around your body with your pointer finger. Then, reach out and explore the edges of your bubble with the palms of your hands by moving them up, down, and around in a circle. Finally, pretend to decorate your bubble and describe how you're decorating it to the children.
3. Now you're going to create your own bubble. Can you show me where it is and describe it to me?
   Pretend to test the edges of the children's bubbles with the palms of your hands.
4. As we play more mindful games together, I'll keep reminding you to check your bubble.

TIPS

1. To help young children develop self-control, ask them to see how close they can get the palms of their hands to your palms without touching. Then ask children to see how close they can get their shoulders to your shoulders without touching, and then their elbows to your elbows. Remind children to be careful not to burst their imaginary bubbles (or yours).

Like *Balloon Arms, Tick-Tock, Zip-Up*, and *Your Own Bubble*, the next game, *Pass the Cup*, is a playful way for young children to build concentration and develop awareness of how their bodies move through space. While encouraging teamwork and coordination, *Pass the Cup* also builds young children's awareness of their bodies as they relate to other people (arms, legs, hands, elbows) and things (tables, chairs, cups of water), as well as awareness of the quality of their movements (sluggish, quick, fluid, jerky). To prepare, fill a small, unbreakable cup with water to about one inch from the rim.

pass the cup

Using teamwork and paying attention to what's happening around us, we pass a cup filled with water without spilling a drop. First we pass it with our eyes open and then with our eyes closed.

LIFE SKILLS Focusing, Caring, Connecting
TARGET AGES Young Children

LEADING THE GAME

1. We're going to pass this cup to one another without spilling any water. What do we have to pay attention to so that the water does not spill? (Looking at the cup and one another, feeling with our hands, moving our arms slowly.)
2. Are you ready? Let's try it.
   Help children silently pass the cup of water back and forth between them two or three times (or around the circle).
3. Now let's see if we can pass the cup with our eyes closed. What types of things will we need to pay attention to if we can't talk or see? (The sound of clothing rustling, the feeling of the person sitting next to us moving, the feeling of the cup in our hands.)
   Help children silently pass the cup with their eyes closed.

TIPS

1. If playing with very young children, pass a closed water bottle first to practice. When children are ready, graduate to passing an open cup.
2. Fill the cup high enough that it's challenging for children to not spill the water, but not too high that they can't be successful at the game.
3. If playing with a group, sit in a circle. After the first round, change the direction you pass the cup.

In the next set of activities, children apply the life skills and themes that they've learned through introspective games to their conversations with friends and family.

hello game

We take turns saying, "Hello" to one another and noticing the color of each other's eyes to help us focus and practice making eye contact.

LIFE SKILLS Focusing, Caring, Connecting
TARGET AGES All Ages

LEADING THE GAME

1. When we look into someone's eyes, we sometimes feel strong feelings—we might feel shy, embarrassed, excited, or happy. And we might feel different every time we do it.
2. Let's try it together now. I'm going to say, "Hello" to you and tell you what color your eyes are, and then you'll have a turn. "Hello, Sara. Your eyes look brown."
3. Now you try.
4. How did it feel?
5. Let's try it again.

TIPS

1. Play the *Hello Game* around the dinner table: "Good evening, Amy. Your eyes look hazel." Or do it first thing in the morning: "Good morning . . ."
2. The wording of the prompt "Your eyes *look*" as opposed to "Your eyes *are*" is deliberate; it allows children to practice observing without analyzing or jumping to a conclusion. As a practical matter, it's common for children to disagree about eye color, and the phrasing of this question eliminates that problem, too.

3. Don't be surprised if young children feel shy at first and cover their eyes, especially if they're playing with new friends or with adults they don't know well. When this happens, describe what you see: "Hello, Alex. Your eyes are covered with your hands!"

The prompt for the *Hello Game* can be changed in countless ways to develop children's awareness of what's happening within and around them and to make the game more interesting for older children. For instance, by asking kids to send one another a friendly wish or to name something or someone they're thankful for, the prompt becomes an expression of the themes of kindness or appreciation. When children ask a question and listen to their friend's response without an agenda, they practice other themes like keeping an open mind and attunement. Here are a few additional *Hello Game* prompts to experiment with:

• Name one thing you are seeing, hearing, tasting, smelling, or touching right now.
• Do you have a friendly wish for yourself? For your friends? For the planet?
• Are you thinking about the past, present, or future right now?
• Is your body language telegraphing what you're thinking and feeling right now to your partner?
• Take a look at your partner's body language and guess what she's thinking and feeling.
• If you could choose a sensory superpower, what would it be? How would you use it to help the world?

Listening with awareness can be difficult, if not impossible, when projections or biases cloud kids' or their parents' perspectives. The next game, *Reflecting Back*, offers several tried-and-true guidelines to help older children, teens, and parents stay on track.

reflecting back

We use these guidelines to help us speak and listen in a helpful and compassionate way.

LIFE SKILLS Focusing, Caring, Connecting
TARGET AGES Older Children, Teens

GUIDELINES FOR REFLECTING BACK

1. We remember that nonverbal cues (tone of voice, gesture, intensity, facial expression) speak volumes and that our body language can send someone a message that we don't intend to send.
2. We listen without imposing our agenda.
3. We notice our biases and internal reactions to what's being said and do our best not to dwell on them.
4. We remind ourselves that it's natural to silently rehearse what we're about to say before we say it and to think about what we said after we've said it. We try not to do either of those things, though, and we do our best to stay in the present.
5. We remind ourselves that silence is a meaningful part of conversation.
6. We remind ourselves that guessing what might be going on in someone else's experience, or comparing our own experiences to theirs, tends not to be as helpful as asking questions.
7. We give ourselves a break when we drift off into our own thoughts or unintentionally direct the conversation toward our own agenda. We remember that the moment we recognize we've been distracted or that the conversation has gotten offtrack is a moment of mindful awareness and an opportunity to begin again.

1. "Nonjudgmental awareness" is an important theme in mindfulness training that is sometimes misunderstood by children and adults. In relational games that emphasize **Caring** and **Connecting**, like the ones in this chapter, we ask kids and parents to suspend judgment and listen to what's being said with an open mind and without jumping to conclusions. This instruction is not a suggestion that they let go of judgments entirely when they practice mindfulness, however. Through games that emphasize **Focusing**, for example, children learn that wisely choosing where to direct their attention in the moment requires *judgment*, and through games that emphasize **Seeing** children learn that it takes *judgment* to navigate the world with wisdom and compassion.

Even with the best intentions, kids can hurt a friend's feelings by blurting something out before they think it through. Pretty much everyone has made this misstep and felt lousy about it later. The sequence of questions in the next game can prevent this from happening and is an example of how I teach children discernment. I learned these questions from Joanie Martin, the retired director of the elementary school at the Crossroads School for Arts & Sciences in Santa Monica, California. When my kids were in the elementary school, she had posted these three questions in the school's entry hall to remind children to speak to one another respectfully.

three gates

We ask ourselves three questions to check that something we are about to say is helpful and kind: *Is it true? Is it necessary? Is it kind?*

LIFE SKILLS Reframing, Caring, Connecting   TARGET AGES All ages

LEADING THE DISCUSSION

1. *Talking points: Sometimes we can hurt someone's feelings even if we don't mean to. How can we know if something we're about to say is respectful? What can we do if we accidentally hurt someone's feelings?*
2. Asking these three questions before we say something is one way to avoid hurting someone's feelings: *Is it true? Is it necessary? Is it kind?*
   Give examples of things you might say, and ask children to help you figure out whether they are kind and respectful by asking the three questions together.
3. *Talking points: When should we ask these questions? Do you ever get a feeling that what you're about to say might not be respectful?*
   Share your personal experiences, and ask children to share theirs.
4. Try asking yourself the three questions next time you get that feeling and tell me what happens.

TIPS

1. Have older children ask a fourth question: *Is it the right time?*
2. Remind children that they don't need to ask these questions every time they speak, only if they catch themselves feeling that what they're about to say may not be helpful.
3. Use *Three Gates* to talk about helpful speech, and use *Is It Helpful?* to talk about helpful actions.

4. The check-ins after relational games like the *Hello Game*, *Reflecting Back*, and *Three Gates* are opportunities to ask children and teens to compare how they feel after they speak and act in a warm-hearted way with how they feel after they act or speak in a way that's angry or unkind. Through check-ins like these, and after playing games like *Friendly Wishes*, *Mind-Body Connection*, and *Mind, Body, Go!* kids can see that their minds and bodies are connected.

Children have an opportunity to reflect on the themes empathy and compassion when they read *Not a Box*, a clever picture book by Antoinette Portis. Before leading the game, make a mental note of how the book is structured: an unidentified narrative voice asks questions on the tan pages, and a bunny answers them on the red pages.

not a box

We pay close attention to the words and pictures in the book *Not a Box* by Antoinette Portis, to understand what the characters are thinking and how they are feeling.

LIFE SKILLS Reframing, Caring, Connecting
TARGET AGES Young Children, Older Children

LEADING THE DISCUSSION
1. Let's read a story together.
   Read the first tan page, where the voice asks the bunny why he's sitting in a box.
2. Who do you think is asking the question?
   Listen to children's responses, then turn to the red page and read, "It's not a box."

3. What is it? How do you think the bunny feels? How do you think the person who's asking the bunny questions feels?

Listen to children's responses and continue reading the questions on the tan pages and the bunny's answers. On each page ask questions like: "What is the box? How is the bunny feeling? What does the bunny want? What does the person asking questions want? How does the person asking questions feel?"

Stop after reading, "It's NOT, NOT, NOT a box."

4. How does the bunny feel now? What does he want? What does the person asking questions want? How do they both feel?

Listen to children's thoughts before turning to the tan page to read the adult's response, "Well, what is it then?"

5. What is it?

Listen to children's responses before turning the page, where there are no words, only a picture of the bunny sitting on the box and thinking.

6. What is the bunny doing?

After listening to children's responses, turn the page to finish the book.

7. *Talking points: Can you tell a story about a time that you didn't see something the same way someone else saw it? Can you tell a story about a time you were misunderstood? Can you tell a story about a time that a misunderstanding corrected itself?*

The phrase "I wonder" is a gentle and effective way to open up a conversation about what it might be like to be in someone else's position. For example, ask a child, "I wonder how your friend is feeling right now" or ask a teenager, "I wonder if there's another way to look at how this happened." Don't forget to view these conversations through a developmental lens. Because children in preschool and early elementary school are still seeing what's happening around them largely through their own perspectives, conversations with young children about caring are most useful if they're placed in the context of the child's own experience. An example of placing something in the context of a child's personal experience is the Golden Rule: "Do unto others as you would have them do unto you."

Even when kids are developmentally able to feel and express empathy in a helpful way, it can be hard for them to do so when their own emotions are unwieldy. Strong, difficult emotions are frequently triggered by what kids think they want, even though they often don't know what they want. (Adults run into the same problem.) For instance, older children and teens might think they want something specific from a friend (an invitation to partner on a project, for instance) when what they actually want is for the friend to hold them in mind and, in doing so, to deepen their connection. The longer kids dwell on the strong negative emotions that come in the wake of not getting what they think they want, the more their perspectives narrow and the less they are able to see what's happening from the other person's point of view. As a result, it becomes more likely that what they don't want will actually come to pass. Through games that highlight **Quieting**, **Focusing**, **Seeing**, **Reframing**, **Caring**, and **Connecting**, kids learn to notice

when they're doing this and shift their perspective to see what's happening from another person's vantage point. Through this wider lens they can come to understand that all of us are interdependent and that everything changes.

The reflections on the themes interdependence and everything changes in the earlier section on **Seeing** served as reminders to older children and teens that what's happening right now is the result of countless factors. Some of the factors are knowable, and some of them are not. As a result, kids can do their research, consider everything they learn with an open mind, and still not have enough information to see and understand another person's situation or point of view. The wordless book *Zoom* by Istvan Banyai demonstrates how easy it is for kids to be mistaken about something or someone if they see only a small part of a much larger picture.

friendly and patient observer

By looking at the pictures in the book *Zoom* by Istvan Banyai, we see that it's easy to jump to the wrong conclusion when we don't have enough information.

LIFE SKILLS Reframing, Caring, Connecting   TARGET AGES All Ages

LEADING THE GAME

1. There are no words in this book, only pictures. Let's take a look.
2. The first page of the book is a picture of reddish-orange shapes that are pointed and have dots on them. There are dots in the space surrounding the shapes, too.
3. What do you think these pointy shapes are? What do you think the dots around the shapes are?
   Listen to children's responses.
4. Are you sure?
   Turn the page to reveal a rooster with dots in the space around it.
5. It looks like it's a rooster. But the dots are still there—what do you think they are?
   Listen to children's responses.
6. Are you sure?
   Turn the page to reveal the rooster standing on something, with two children watching him from a window.

7. Do you think the children are inside or outside? How about the rooster? Is it inside or outside? The dots are still in the picture—what do you think they are?

Listen to children's responses.

8. Are you sure?

Continue turning pages and asking questions in this pattern until it's revealed that all of the images so far—the rooster, the children, and the farm—are toys. The dots have disappeared from the image without an explanation.

9. What is it after all? What happened to the dots?

Listen to children's responses.

10. Are you sure?

Keep paging through the book and asking questions in this pattern until you reach the end.

11. *Talking points: Tell a story about a time when you or someone else jumped to a conclusion without much information. Was your conclusion correct? Why do you think it was or wasn't correct?*

To make seeing the big picture even more difficult, what kids and parents see, think, and hear is influenced by what's happened in their own lives. Parents project their hopes, fears, biases, and values onto their kids' experiences, and kids project their hopes, fears, biases, and values right back onto their parents' experiences. This interconnected, always changing web of perceptions and projections means that no one can ever know or feel the entirety of another person's experience. But if parents and their kids try to look at what's happening from the other person's perspective and with an open mind, they can come pretty close. This practical understanding of the themes an open mind, interdependence, everything changes, and clarity leads to acceptance, another theme that's central to a wise and compassionate worldview.

That we don't know and can't control every factor that informs other people's actions is relatively easy to accept. It's often more difficult to accept that we don't know and can't control all the factors that inform our own actions, either. This is as true for our kids as it is for us. There will always be seemingly perfect parents who look like they have it more together than we do. From the outside they seem to pack the perfect lunches, plan the perfect birthday parties, and organize the perfect cultural adventures. Acceptance gives us the space to step back, drop our preconceived notions of the ideal parent, and look at the big picture with an open mind. When we do, we recognize that everyone is limited in what he or she can do, including the seemingly perfect parents, and including us. This obvious fact of life can be remarkably elusive, and accepting it can be hard to do. Many of us find acceptance to be easier when we remind ourselves that being comfortable in our own skin is a far better form of modeling than trying to twist ourselves into metaphorical pretzels to be like somebody else. The motto of the good-enough parent might well be the one I saw written on the lime-green Post-it that my daughter stuck to the edge of her bookshelf years ago: *esse qualm videri*, "to be, rather than to seem."

—— 13 ——

FREEDOM

A wise old hummingbird riding a bicycle comes upon a young hummingbird lying on her back, the soles of her feet facing the sky. "What are you doing with your feet in the air?" asks the old hummingbird.

The young one replies, "I heard the sky is going to fall today."

The older hummingbird scratches his head. "Do you think one small bird with spindly legs can keep the sky from falling?"

"I could use some help," says the young one. The wise hummingbird shrugs, lies next to her, and points the soles of his feet to the sky, too. They pass the time laughing and joking until an enormous, cranky elephant interrupts to tell them they're wasting their time. The two new friends pay no attention.

Another hummingbird shows up and joins the first two. Then a fourth appears, and a fifth, and a sixth, until soon there's a long line of spindly-legged hummingbirds with the soles of their tiny feet facing the sky, laughing, singing, and telling stories.

As night falls, the elephant returns. "See, nothing happened. This was all a waste of time." But the first bird has a different perspective. "It worked," she cries, jumping up and brushing herself off. "Congratulations, everyone."

Their goal achieved, the newly minted team of hummingbirds declares the day a remarkable success. In groups of twos and threes, they fly back to their nests and make plans to have dinner, get some sleep, and meet up tomorrow to save the world again.

Does the wise old hummingbird think he is helping the young one save the world, or is he keeping her company to be kind? It's tough for anyone other than the old bird to know his motivation, but kindness is good for the health and well-being of both the giver and the receiver. In *The How of Happiness*, Dr. Sonja Lyubomirsky, a professor at University of California, Riverside, explains that kindness connects the giver with other people, and consequently, givers see positive qualities in receivers that they hadn't seen before. Acts of kindness inspire other people to be kind as well, while boosting their self-image because they feel altruistic and generous. Acts of agenda-less kindness needn't be anonymous nor grand. The most meaningful ones are often small and targeted toward solving a specific problem, like offering jumper cables to a stranger whose car battery needs a charge or helping a fellow passenger lift a heavy bag into the overhead bin on an airplane.

For centuries meditators have practiced secretly doing something nice for someone else by silently wishing him or her well. The next game is an active, age-appropriate adaptation of this classical kindness practice.

wishes for the world

We pretend to make a giant ball that holds all of our friendly wishes for the world. We toss the ball up into the sky together and imagine that it carries our friendly wishes to everyone, everywhere.

LIFE SKILLS Focusing, Caring, Connecting
TARGET AGES Young Children, Older Children

1. *Talking points: What does it mean to visualize or imagine something? What are friendly wishes?*

2. We're going to imagine that we're sending our friendly wishes to the world in a big, floating ball.

3. Let's start by pretending to hold the ball together. Put your hands out and help me hold the ball, like this.

4. What does the ball look like? What color is it? Is it sparkly? Does it have polka dots or stripes? Close your eyes and see if you can picture it.

5. Now we'll take turns putting our friendly wishes in the ball. Who has a friendly wish for the world?
   Help children name their wishes and mime putting them in the ball. Explain that with each wish, the ball gets bigger and heavier.

6. Let's count to three and then throw the ball up into the sky together: one, two, three. Wave good-bye and imagine that the ball is bringing our wishes to everyone, everywhere.

Regardless of whether kids and families are acting in service of a goal, in response to a conflict, or altruistically, the themes and life skills they develop through mindfulness and meditation offer a framework for acting with wisdom and compassion in any situation:

- First, check your motivation.
- Then, do your research.
- Look at the big picture with an open mind.
- Choose how to respond, then let the music play.
- Afterward, reflect on what happened and work through any anger or hurt feelings.

Check Your Motivation

Through games that explore the theme interdependence, children see that countless factors lead up to every choice they make, and most of these factors are outside of their control. Motivation, another universal theme, is one factor that kids can control. Like the hummingbird from the start of this chapter, the little boy from *The Carrot Seed*, the blue engine from *The Little Engine That Could*, and Lion from *The Lion and the Bird*, children can prioritize kindness over results. Prioritizing kindness doesn't mean kids put other people's needs ahead of their own; it means that they keep both other people and themselves in mind when they make decisions, speak, and act. Nor does prioritizing kindness mean that children pay no attention to results. Results are important, and so is being realistic, which is what kids are being when they accept that some things are out of their control.

Like human's closest living relatives, chimpanzees and bonobo apes, kids are hardwired for survival, and interpersonal conflict is inevitable. Even acts of agenda-less kindness are not always received in the spirit in which they are intended, and nice kids get hurt. On playgrounds and in middle-school lunchrooms, well-intentioned children are bullies' targets, especially if they're perceived as being unable or unwilling to defend themselves. The themes that run through a wise and compassionate worldview help children and teens to identify what's important to them and to recognize when a friend's behavior is out-of-bounds. Kids learn to stand up for what matters and to stand up for themselves by developing the life skills **Quieting**, **Focusing**, **Seeing**, **Reframing**, **Caring**, and **Connecting**.

Do Your Research

To respond skillfully to a complex situation, children start by reflecting on their own role along with the roles of everyone involved and then on the role of the system in which the situation is embedded. *Five Whys*, a game I learned from the meditation teacher and author Ken McLeod, offers older children and teens a framework through which to look at these various roles. This game can be played in pairs, with one child asking questions and the other child answering them, or in a group, with children writing their answers down. When playing with a group, give each child a piece of paper and pencil.

five whys

We ask the question "Why?" five times to help us understand a problem and its solution.

LIFE SKILLS Reframing, Caring, Connecting
TARGET AGES Older Children, Teens

LEADING THE GAME

1. Think of a complicated situation that you've dealt with in the past.
2. What was your role in this situation? Answer in one or two sentences.
   Wait for children to write their answers down (or to respond to their partners).
3. Now, turn your response into a "why" question. For instance, if your answer is "My role was to solve a problem," ask, "Why was I responsible for solving the problem?" Then briefly answer.
   Guide children in continuing to ask and answer "why" questions for as long as they find the questions helpful, but no fewer than five times.
   Reframe the prompt to inquire about other people's roles, and finally the system's role, in the situation. This might seem like a lot of questions, but asking and answering them moves quickly.

Look at the Big Picture with an Open Mind

Once kids have identified the various roles that people play in a situation, they're able to focus on what everyone has in common rather than on their differences.

three things in common

When we have a disagreement or misunderstanding or if someone simply gets on our nerves, we acknowledge our feelings and think of three things we have in common.

LIFE SKILLS Reframing, Caring, Connecting   TARGET AGES All Ages

LEADING THE DISCUSSION

1. Think of someone who you've had a disagreement with or who gets on your nerves.
2. How do you feel about him or her? How do you think he or she feels about you?
3. I bet you both have something in common, too. Quickly name three things you have in common.

TIPS

1. Remind children that the people we love most might also be the ones who annoy us the most. This can be a remarkably helpful shift in perspective for kids with siblings who get on their nerves.
2. *Friendly Wishes for Difficult People* is a useful companion game to *Three Things in Common*. Remember, the goal of both games is to help children broaden their perspectives, not to change the way they feel about a person they find difficult.

The games *Five Whys*, *Three Things in Common*, and *Not a Box* can easily morph into conversations that explore interdependence and how everything changes. Viewing actions through the lens of these two themes is a powerful reminder to older kids that whatever is happening—good, bad, or neutral—is not entirely about them and will change. In *Stadium Wave* and *Pass the Pulse*, children experience interdependence directly.

stadium wave

We use teamwork to coordinate our movements and create the illusion of a wave.

LIFE SKILLS Focusing, Seeing, Connecting
TARGET AGES All Ages

LEADING THE GAME

1. Can anyone describe a stadium wave? (When people stand up or raise their arms in turn to create a movement that looks like a wave moving through the ocean.)
   Help children form a line or a circle and show them the direction in which the wave will move. Then choose a child to begin the wave.
2. Crouch down, with your knees bent and your hands touching the floor, like this.
   Demonstrate the starting position and movement. Then explain that the second player will start when the first person has his hands in the air, and so on.
3. When I say, "Go," start the wave.
4. Let's speed it up!
5. Let's switch directions.
6. Let's try slowing it down, too.

In *Stadium Wave* children practice teamwork by coordinating their movements to achieve a common goal. The same holds true in *Pass the Pulse*, where friends send a pulse of energy around a circle by squeezing one another's hands in turn. To prepare, help children sit in a circle and hold hands. Then choose a child to begin.

pass the pulse

We use teamwork to coordinate our movements and send a pulse of energy all the way around the circle.

LIFE SKILLS Focusing, Caring, Connecting   TARGET AGES All Ages

LEADING THE GAME

1. When I say, "Go," gently squeeze the hand of the person holding your left hand.
2. When you feel your right hand get a squeeze, that's your cue to gently squeeze your left hand and pass the pulse to the next person.
3. Let's speed it up.
4. Switch directions.
5. Slow it down.

Choose How to Respond, Then Let the Music Play

The person who responds to a conflict determines its course, not the one who initiates it. To ensure that their responses are wise and compassionate, older kids revisit their motivation, review their research with an open mind, and respond as best they can based on the information they have. Since no one can uncover each and every factor embedded in the infinite web of changing causes and conditions that lead up to a decision, whatever choice kids make will be a bit like shooting in the dark. That needn't discourage children, though. If it does, remind them of the Dalai Lama's advice from *Beyond Religion*: "It is important to acknowledge [that no matter how hard we try, we won't be able to see the whole picture], but it should not worry us. . . . Instead it should temper our actions with proper humility and caution."

There are times when the wise and compassionate response is not to engage, and other times when the wise and compassionate response is to act. When the most skillful response is to do nothing, I encourage older kids to let the music play, and remind them that misunderstandings often correct themselves when we allow a situation to play itself out. The themes that children explore through mindfulness and meditation help them discern whether their best response to a misunderstanding is to step up and try to correct the confusion or to step back and leave it alone. When the wise and compassionate response is to correct the confusion, kids will sometimes have to stand up for what they believe in. The life skills **Quieting, Focusing, Seeing, Reframing, Caring,** and **Connecting** give them the capacity to do so with the inner calm of a Japanese tea master, like the one in this story of long ago:

A high-ranking samurai is impressed by his tea master's serene concentration and bestows upon him the robes and rank of a samurai. Later, the tea master meets a visiting samurai warrior who, after sizing him up, asks why he's wearing robes. The tea master explains, but the warrior won't have it: "If you wear the robes of the samurai, you must fight like a samurai." He challenges the tea master to a duel the next morning.

The tea master is determined to defend his own honor and the honor of the samurai who gave him the robes. He finds a fencing master and, trembling with fear, asks to learn how to fight. The fencing master agrees to teach him, provided the tea master performs one last ceremony. In preparation for the ritual, the tea master concentrates calmly on the exquisite cups, pots, and tea leaves, and his fears fall away. The fencing master drinks his cup of tea and offers this advice: "Approach the duel as if you are preparing for a tea ceremony, and you'll be ready for combat."

The tea master prepares for the duel with the serene concentration of preparing for a tea ceremony, and his fears fall away once again. He draws his sword and holds it high above his head. His opponent bows in response, recognizing that the tea master is a samurai after all.

Reflect on What Happened and Work Through Any Anger or Hurt Feelings

The tea master let the music play, the misunderstanding corrected itself, and his story came to a happy ending. Unfortunately, that's not always the case. Even when kids do everything right, they can still get hurt, bringing them back full circle to Dr. Seuss's version of the first insight of mindfulness: "I'm sorry to say so / but, sadly, it's true / that Bang-ups and Hang-ups / *can* happen to you." When working through suffering, it's important that children learn to acknowledge it and let it go. In the next game, children let go of misunderstandings, anger, and other painful feelings by picturing their hang-ups and bang-ups inside of pink bubbles and watching them float away. The most powerful part of this game is when children wave good-bye to their anger and old hurts, wishing them well.

pink bubble

We imagine that a disappointment or another feeling that is bothering us is inside a pink bubble. As it floats away, we wave good-bye and wish it well.

LIFE SKILLS Focusing, Quieting, Caring
TARGET AGES All Ages

1. Sit with your back straight and your body relaxed, resting your hands gently on your knees. Close your eyes, and let's take a few breaths together.

2. Think of a disappointment or a feeling that's bothering you and put it inside an imaginary pink bubble.

3. In your mind, watch the light, airy, pink bubble float away and imagine that whatever is bothering you is floating away with it.

4. Wave good-bye and wish it well.

5. *Talking points: What types of things bother you? How did it feel to let go of something that was bothering you? How did it feel to wish it well? Is there anything else you'd like to let go of and wish well?*

When children feel angry and upset, they can become preoccupied with their own concerns. Then their perspectives narrow, and it becomes difficult for them to see what's happening from another person's point of view. Kids can turn a narrow mind-set around by pulling back and looking at a situation within the wider context of the themes we've explored in this book. With more space in their heads, they can reflect on what's happening with an open mind and wonder whether the person who hurt their feelings is hurting, too. After all, he or she wants to be happy, safe, and secure, just like they do. Reflections like these make it easier for kids to have empathy and compassion for others and to have self-compassion, too. From this vantage point, children have more clarity and can see that whatever is happening is changing, interdependent, and the result of countless causes and conditions (cause and effect). With this more balanced view they are better able to accept that bad things happen to everyone and appreciate that good things happen, too. An appreciation feedback loop can then emerge: the more thankful children feel, the happier they become, and the happier children become, the more thankful they feel.

The next game encourages children to pull back and view their challenges through this more spacious mind-set. Children roll a small ball back and forth while naming things that bother them along with things that make them happy. It can be played with a partner or with a group sitting in a circle.

still i feel lucky

As we roll a ball back and forth, we name things that bother us and things that make us happy.

LIFE SKILLS Seeing, Reframing   TARGET AGES All Ages

LEADING THE GAME

1. We're going to roll this ball to one another, and when it's your turn, name one thing that's bothering you. Then roll the ball and say something positive about the same topic.
2. I'll go first. "I have to study tonight instead of going to the game." *Roll the ball to another child while saying, "Still, I feel lucky for all the other times I got to go to the game."*
3. Now you name something and roll the ball back. (For example, "My little sister was annoying me today. Still, I feel lucky to have my sister.")
Guide children in speeding up the pace as the play continues.

When bang-ups, hang-ups, misunderstandings, and hurt feelings happen, the themes threaded through a wise and compassionate worldview encourage kids to dig deep and remember their motivation. Dzogchen Ponlop Rinpoche, a meditation teacher known for making ancient Eastern wisdom accessible to those in the West, explains in his book *Rebel Buddha*: "So this becomes a true test of how serious we are and how far we're willing to go. Can we stick to our altruistic motivation when we're being attacked by someone we intended to help? When we feel vulnerable and exposed to the judgments of others, do we revert to a strategy of preemptive strikes? It's not one big battle we're facing that will decide everything; it's the most simple and commonplace encounters in our daily life that test our courage and willingness to open our heart fearlessly. . . . Sometimes we'll succeed and sometimes we'll fail, but as long as we keep coming back to our original intention, that's the essence of transcendent practice." This transcendent practice has been offered as a pathway to freedom for centuries.

Freedom isn't flashy. Most of the time freedom looks like the quiet constancy that's modeled by the lion, the old hummingbird, the little blue engine, and the little boy who planted a carrot seed. In the commencement speech at Kenyon College in which David Foster Wallace told his fish story (the one I retold in section 2), he also told graduates: "There are all different kinds of freedom, and the kind that is most precious you will not hear much talked about in the great outside world of winning and achieving and displaying. The really important kind of freedom involves attention, and awareness, and discipline, and effort, and being able truly to care about other people and to sacrifice for them, over and over, in myriad petty little unsexy ways, every day."

The path to freedom through mindfulness and meditation requires the attention, awareness, discipline, effort, and sacrifice that Wallace points to in his commencement speech, along with the other themes we've been reflecting on in this book. I wouldn't describe this path as about "winning and achieving and displaying," and sometimes it has worn me down. It has also been exhilarating, though. And it has offered me a degree of psychological freedom that I hadn't thought possible by showing me that there's mystery and joy just waiting to be discovered in every breath, with every step, and in every moment. For that, I'll be forever grateful.

PARTING
THOUGHTS

It might feel like this book contains an overwhelming amount of information, especially for someone new to mindfulness and meditation. That's why I'm leaving you with a short list of tips together with a section in which I answer frequently asked questions. But before moving ahead to Tips and FAQs I'd like to pause and offer a suggestion: keep in mind the power of stories when sharing mindfulness and meditation with children and families, especially when sharing ideas that are difficult to put into words.

If you're new to storytelling, a good starting point is your child's bookshelf, especially picture books that teach the universal themes you've been reflecting on while playing mindful games. (A table of themes is at the end of the book.) As you become familiar with them, you'll start to see universal themes embedded in the everyday questions that challenge you, and in the mysteries in life that are hard to understand. Your challenges and mysteries will then become fodder for your own stories with a trip to the supermarket, picking up your kids at school, and refereeing a misunderstanding between tired and fussy siblings, all yielding lessons in mindfulness. Stories like these, that are drawn from your family's experiences, are especially powerful because they have a level of immediacy and authenticity that can't be replicated. The best part? Each day is full of them!

Tips for Leading Mindful Games

• Find a relatively quiet place where you can sit or lie down comfortably, without being disturbed.

• Before leading a game, get a feel for it by going through the steps on your own.

• Use your regular speaking voice, and your own words, when you lead a game.

• Some children are so determined to concentrate that they tense their muscles when they meditate. Others are so relaxed that they curl up and fall asleep. From time to time, remind kids to keep their backs straight and their bodies relaxed.

• Remind children that there is no right or wrong way to feel.

• Sometimes children are uncomfortable closing their eyes, even when the game they're playing is easier with eyes closed. Don't insist that children close their eyes, but it's helpful to remind them that you'll keep your eyes open and watch the room.

• Children will respond to the games differently, and games that come naturally to some kids might be difficult for others. There's no reason to force a child to play if he feels uncomfortable. Just switch to another game that explores similar life skills and themes.

• All of the games include mindfulness-based strategies that are useful to everyone, regardless of age. Don't be surprised when older children and teens are drawn to activities meant for young children, and young children have fun playing games that seem over their heads.

Do you have an elevator pitch that describes mindfulness?

The best-known shorthand definition of mindfulness comes from Jon Kabat-Zinn's MBSR: paying attention, on purpose, in the present moment, without judgment.

How do kids pay attention to their thoughts and feelings without judgment?

When children notice how they feel, we hope they'll use a kind inner voice that sounds something like this: "It's really hard to sit still right now, and that's OK. Everyone feels this way sometimes. I can sit here, feeling my body and all the energy I have—my breath moving fast, my heart beating quickly—I can take a breath, listen to sounds, become aware of how I feel, and be OK."

What's the difference between mindfulness and meditation?

In the ancient languages Sanskrit and Pali the word *mindfulness* is defined as "remembering," as in remembering our object of attention. The word *meditation* is defined in different ways among contemplative traditions, but in the Tibetan language the word for meditation means "familiarization," as in familiarizing ourselves with the activity in our minds. Here's a shorthand way to differentiate between the two: *Meditation* is a method through which we familiarize ourselves with our minds by working with them directly, and *mindfulness* is knowing where our mind is, and our state of mind, in the present moment.

Will mindfulness help kids calm down?

We want children to notice how they're feeling in the moment, not to change the way they feel. When approached in this way, mindfulness often helps children feel calmer and more relaxed, but not always.

What's the difference between "feeling your breathing" and "noticing your breathing"?

Encouraging kids to feel their breathing (rather than to notice it) is one way to orient a mindful game away from thinking and toward sensory experiences.

FAQs: How to Start Playing Mindful Games with Kids

How do I get started?

A good place to begin is with child-friendly versions of the mindfulness practices that you enjoy and find helpful. If mindful listening resonates with you, start by leading kids in mindful listening games like *Fading Tone, What Did I Hear?* and *Counting Sounds.*

I don't have much time and am new to meditation; how do I get started?

Spend the time you have on your own mindfulness and meditation practice. Start with brief and frequent moments of awareness—like *I Stop and Feel My Breathing* and *Resting and Noticing*—where you gently look at life experiences with the intention to understand them, not to judge or change them. Brief and frequent moments of awareness like these can create meaningful shifts in your behavior and mind-set relatively quickly. These shifts make it easier to lead mindful games, and to understand the themes and life skills woven through them.

I have some experience with mindfulness and meditation but not a lot of it; how do I get started?

Kids have an uncanny ability to sniff out what's real and discount what's fake, but you'll be OK if you teach what's real for you. For instance, if stopping and feeling your breathing helps steady your mind and heart, share that strategy with children. If shifting your attention to a sensory experience in the present moment helps dampen your worries and anxieties, share that strategy with children.

FAQs: How to Lead Mindful Games

How long and how often is enough?

Children don't need to practice mindfulness for a long time for it to be helpful; they just need to be consistent. Frequently integrate brief moments of awareness into daily life, and don't forget that repetition is important.

Should children meditate every day?

It's fantastic when kids practice formal, sitting meditation everyday. Encourage kids to give it a try, but never insist that they meditate.

How can I help kids integrate mindfulness into their daily lives?

Frequently interrupt children's routines to pause for a brief moment of awareness. For instance, ask a child to notice what the doorknob feels like against his hand when he opens the door, or to put his socks on in slow motion. Instead of hollering "Watch where you're going!" when a child bumps into someone or something, ask her to "Stop and feel her breathing for a moment" or to "Move slowly like a sloth."

How can I get kids to talk about mindfulness and meditation?

It's helpful to check in with kids after they play a mindful game so they can tell you about their experience and how they feel. As a rule of thumb, put as few words as possible between the game and children's opportunity to describe how they feel.

What are Talking Points?

Talking Points are included in the instructions for many of the games. They're designed to jump-start a conversation about the themes and life skills children explore when they play the games, and how those themes and life skills can be helpful in kids' daily lives. You don't need to ask and answer all of the Talking Points that are listed in the instructions, and feel free to replace our Talking Points with your own.

FAQs: How to Navigate Obstacles

How do I get kids to buy into mindfulness?

Invite young children to lead more active mindful games—like *Zip-Up, Slowly, Slowly,* and *Balloon Arms.* Besides helping with buy-in, leading a game can help children build confidence, and, if they're playing with other children, leading gives kids a chance to practice speaking in front of a group.

Encourage older children and teens to practice brief and frequent moments of awareness by playing games like *Feeling My Feet, Mindful Waiting,* and *One Bite at a Time.*

What do I say to children who feel frustrated and that mindfulness "isn't working"?

It's often helpful to tell children stories about your own challenges with mindfulness and meditation (we've all had them). Make sure you share only basic, relatively minor, challenges and stay away from talking to children about larger, more serious problems. This is an important point because we don't want to inadvertently send kids a message that we want them to take care of us, rather than the other way around.

What if children are disruptive?

When it's hard for children to control their bodies and/or voices, ask them to take a break until they're able to speak and act respectfully. Remind them that they're welcome to participate again when they're ready. Some games and activities, especially those that require concentration, can be frustrating, and it makes sense that every now and again kids will need a break.

What if a child raises a sensitive topic at an inappropriate time or place?

Acknowledge the child's concern, then shift the tone and the subject matter of the conversation. Be sure to revisit the topic with the child privately later.

ACKNOWLEDGMENTS

With deep appreciation to Annaka Harris, whose role in this book, and the companion set of cards that follow, went far beyond that of an editor. She and I would like to thank Amy Rennert, our agent, for shepherding this project through to publication; Cortland Dahl, Sue Smalley, Sam Harris, Anna McDonnell, and Seth Greenland for reading and commenting on early drafts; Mark Greenberg, Joseph Goldstein, Surya Das, Trudy Goodman, Carolyn Gimian, Jim Gimian, Barry Boyce, Steve Hickman, Mark Bertin, and Tandy Parks for answering questions and tossing ideas around with us; and Diana Winston, Martin Matzinger, and Mira Matzinger for sharing their daughter Mira's game. *Mindful Games* is far richer, and frankly better, because of the wise and insightful contributions from these close colleagues and friends.

Thank you to Lindsay duPont for her playful drawings, and to Suzi Tortora for her early help in weaving movement into several of these games, especially those for young children.

To Beth Frankl, and the team at Shambhala Publications, thank you for helping me keep an eye on the broadest possible audience for this book, and for your patience and encouragement.

This book is a synthesis of more than eight hundred pages of manuals that I developed over the span of close to a decade while training parents, teachers, and clinicians in how to share secular mindfulness with children and families. More people have offered me support throughout this process than I could possibly name, but here are a few who I'd like to single out:

To the remarkable meditation teachers who graciously agreed to serve as advisors to the Inner Kids professional training program— Jack Kornfield, Sharon Salzberg, Surya Das, B. Alan Wallace, Gay MacDonald, Trudy Goodman, and Diana Winston. I deeply appreciate, and feel honored by, your support of this work.

To my exceptional teaching compatriots in the various Inner Kids trainings—Daniela Labra, Ryan Redman, Daniel Rechtshaffen, and Tandy Parks. Thank you for your friendship, good humor, and commitment to practice.

Thanks to Michelle Limantour, Nick Seaver, Lisa Henson, Sue Smalley, Charlie Stanford, Shelly Sowell, Jenny Manriguez, Deb Walsh, Mary Sweet, and Melissa Baker for your help during the formative stages of the development of the Inner Kids program.

To those who have participated in an Inner Kids training and who are now taking this work forward and making it their own, a sincere thank-you for your energy sharing mindfulness with children, teens, and families.

Last, I wish to express my appreciation to all of my teachers for their warmth, care, and instruction, with special thanks to two remarkable brothers whose teaching has inspired me in ways that are tough to articulate yet meaningful beyond measure—Tsoknyi Rinpoche and Yongey Mingyur Rinpoche.

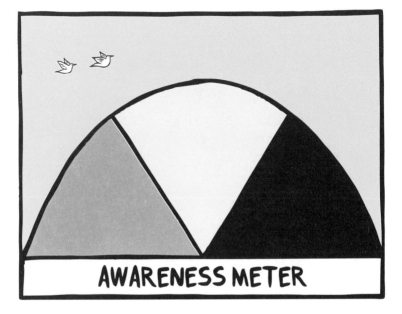

AWARENESS METER

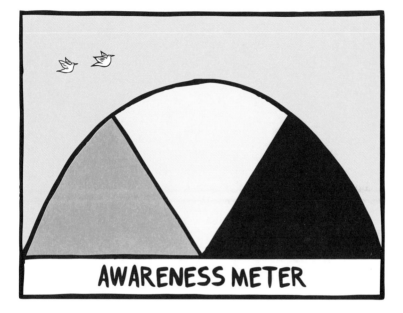

AWARENESS METER

TABLE OF THEMES

In the following table of themes, I included the phrase "I remind myself" in each description as a nod to the remembering function of mindfulness. Reminding children of the themes acceptance, appreciation, or attention, for example, feels more consistent with the practice of mindfulness and meditation than telling them to speak and act in a particular way.

Acceptance I remind myself that I can't know or control every cause or condition that leads up to this moment. My motivation is one thing that I can control, though, and I can do my best to speak and act in a way that's wise and compassionate.	**Appreciation** When I remember to appreciate my relationships, health, good experiences, belongings, and the natural world, I remind myself that appreciation is a cause and effect of happiness.
Attention (the Floodlight) I remind myself that I can hold back from reacting to what's happening within and around me so that I can investigate it with an open mind.	**Attention (the Spotlight)** I remind myself that I can choose where to place my attention and that I can keep it there.
Attunement I remind myself that I can watch, listen, sense, interpret, and respond to what other people say and do so that I can see and understand them, and they can feel seen and understood.	**Cause and Effect** I remind myself that what I do and say will affect other people and the planet, and what other people say and do will affect the planet and me.

Clarity

To see what's happening within and around me clearly, I remind myself to step back and take a look at the big picture with an open mind and without jumping to conclusions.

Compassion

I remind myself that I have the capacity to understand what something looks and feels like from another person's perspective and to respond to him or her wisely and with kindness.

Wise Confidence

I remind myself that I can tolerate uncomfortable situations and feelings and that I can stay clearheaded and warmhearted in any situation.

Discernment

Before responding to or judging a complex situation, I remind myself to consider whether what's happening and my possible response are helpful to other people, the planet, and me.

Empathy

I remind myself that I can step back from any situation, view it from another person's perspective, and imagine how he or she feels.

Everything Changes

I remind myself that everything comes, everything goes, and everything is in flux.

Interdependence

I remind myself that what's happening in this moment is the result of countless interdependent factors, some of which I know, some of which I don't know, and some of which are entirely outside of my control.

Joy

I remind myself that the conditions for joy and happiness are here all the time, happening all by themselves, and that I can tap into them at any time.

Kindness

I remind myself to focus more on the goodness of what I'm doing than on the results.

Motivation

I remind myself to reflect on why I'm about to do or say something before I do or say it, to make sure that my purpose is wise and compassionate.

An Open Mind I remind myself that even things that seem different from one another have something in common and that there is more than one side to every story.	**Patience** I remind myself that it often takes time to see the results of my own and other peoples' efforts.
Present Moment I remind myself that I can resist getting sidetracked from the present so that I can observe, listen, and be fully engaged in what's happening right now.	**Restraint (Behavioral)** I remind myself that I can compose myself even when I feel stressed, overly excited, or upset, and I can hold back from reacting to a situation before thinking it through.
Restraint (Contemplative) I remind myself that I can tolerate strong emotions and hold back from reacting to my thoughts, feelings, and sensations.	**Self-Compassion** I remind myself to view what I think, feel, say, and do through a wise and kind perspective and to respond to my own thoughts and feelings with wisdom and kindness, too.

INDEX OF GAMES

REFERENCES

Part One: Quieting

Introduction

"Goldilocks and the Three Bears" is based on a British folk story.

Siegel, Daniel J. *The Developing Mind: Toward a Neurobiology of Interpersonal Experience.* New York: Guilford, 1999.

Hanson, Rick, and Richard Mendius. *Buddha's Brain: The Practical Neuroscience of Happiness, Love, and Wisdom.* Oakland, CA: New Harbinger Publications, 2009.

1. Breathing on Purpose

The Christopher Robin quote is widely attributed to A. A. Milne, but it appears to be from a Disney movie, *Pooh's Grand Adventure: The Search for Christopher Robin.* The sentiments are based on similar concepts in the original Winnie-the-Pooh books by Milne.

Goleman, Daniel. *Emotional Intelligence.* New York: Bantam, 1995.

Tortora, Suzi. *The Dancing Dialogue: Using the Communicative Power of Movement with Young Children.* Baltimore: Paul H. Brookes, 2006.

2. Anchors for Attention

Neff, Kristin, and Christopher Germer. *Mindful Self-Compassion.* Accessed January 7, 2016. www.mindfulselfcompassion.org.

Germer, Christopher K. *The Mindful Path to Self-Compassion: Freeing Yourself from Destructive Thoughts and Emotions.* New York: Guilford, 2009.

Levine, Peter A., and Maggie Kline. *Trauma-Proofing Your Kids: A Parents' Guide for Instilling Confidence, Joy, and Resilience.* Berkeley, CA: North Atlantic, 2008.

Tsokyni Rinpoche and Eric Swanson. *Open Heart, Open Mind: Awakening the Power of Essence Love.* New York: Harmony, 2012.

Tsokyni Rinpoche. "How to Drop into Your Body and Feelings." *Lion's Roar,* August 24, 2015.

Part Two: Seeing and Reframing

Introduction

Wallace, David Foster. *This Is Water: Some Thoughts, Delivered on a Significant Occasion, about Living a Compassionate Life.* New York: Little, Brown, 2009.

3. An Open Mind

The story about a father, his son, and a horse is based on a Chinese folk tale.

Goldstein, Joseph. "One Dharma." On "*The Buddha*: A Film by David Grubin" web page, *PBS*, April 20, 2010. Accessed January 7, 2016. www.pbs.org/thebuddha/blog/2010/apr/20/one-dharma-joseph-goldstein/.

Kabat-Zinn, Myla, and Jon Kabat-Zinn. *Everyday Blessings: The Inner Work of Mindful Parenting.* New York: Hyperion, 1997.

His Holiness the Dalai Lama. *Beyond Religion: Ethics for a Whole World.* Boston: Houghton Mifflin Harcourt, 2011.

Harris, Annaka. *I Wonder.* Illustrated by John Rowe. Los Angeles: Four Elephants, 2013.

Rosenthal, Amy Krouse, and Tom Lichtenheld. *Duck! Rabbit!* San Francisco: Chronicle, 2009.

4. Appreciation

Seuss, Dr. *Oh, the Places You'll Go!* New York: Random House, 1990.

The story of the monkey and the hunter's trap is based on "Makkata Sutta: The Foolish Monkey." Translated by Andrew Olendzki. *Access to Insight*, 2005. Accessed January 18, 2016. www.accesstoinsight.org/tipitaka/sn/sn47/sn47.007.olen.html.

Iyer, Pico. "The Value of Suffering." Editorial. *New York Times*, September 8, 2013.

Baraz, James. "Frame It with Gratitude." *Huffington Post*, May 3, 2010. Accessed January 7, 2016. www.huffingtonpost.com/james-baraz /frame-it-with-gratitude_b_484722.html.

5. What's Happening Now

Harris, Dan. *10% Happier: How I Tamed the Voice in My Head, Reduced Stress without Losing My Edge, and Found Self-Help That Actually Works; A True Story.* New York: HarperCollins, 2014.

Ricard, Matthieu. *Happiness: A Guide to Developing Life's Most Important Skill.* New York: Little, Brown, 2006.

Dahl, Cortland J., Antoine Lutz, and Richard J. Davidson. "Reconstructing and Deconstructing the Self: Cognitive Mechanisms in Meditation Practice." *Trends in Cognitive Sciences* 19, no. 9 (2015): 515–23.

Greenberg, Mark. Personal interview, January 2, 2016.

Dahl, Cortland J. Personal interview, January 2, 2016.

Portis, Antoinette. *Wait.* New York: Roaring Brook, 2015.

Hanh, Thich Nhat. "Five Steps to Mindfulness." *Mindful*, August 23, 2010.

Kornfield, Jack. *The Wise Heart: A Guide to the Universal Teachings of Buddhist Psychology.* New York: Bantam, 2008.

Killingsworth, Matthew A., and Daniel T. Gilbert. "A Wandering Mind Is an Unhappy Mind." *Science* 330, no. 6006 (2010): 932.

Smalley, Susan. Personal interview, January 1, 2016.

Sapolsky, Robert M. "The Benefits of Mind-Wandering." *Wall Street Journal*, June 19, 2015.

Part Three: Focusing

Introduction

Krauss, Ruth. *The Carrot Seed.* Illustrated by Crockett Johnson. New York: Harper & Brothers, 1945.

Mingyur, Yongey, Rinpoche, and Eric Swanson. *The Joy of Living: Unlocking the Secret and Science of Happiness.* New York: Harmony, 2007.

Salzberg, Sharon. *Real Happiness: The Power of Meditation; A 28-Day Program.* New York: Workman, 2011.

Piper, Watty. *The Little Engine That Could.* Illustrated by Lois Lenski. New York: Philomel, 2005.

6. Mindful Breathing

Chödrön, Pema. *The Wisdom of No Escape and the Path of Loving-Kindness.* Boston: Shambhala, 1991.

Chödrön, Pema, and Joan Duncan Oliver. *Living Beautifully with Uncertainty and Change.* Boston: Shambhala, 2012.

Wallace, B. Alan. *Genuine Happiness: Meditation as the Path to Fulfillment.* Hoboken, NJ: John Wiley & Sons, 2005.

———. Personal interview, May 2, 2012.

7. Spotlight of Attention

Olendzki, Andrew. "Mindfulness and Meditation." In *Clinical Handbook of Mindfulness*, edited by Fabrizio Didonna, 37–44. New York: Springer, 2009.

Gimian, Carolyn Rose. Personal interview, December 16, 2015.

Flook, Lisa, Susan L. Smalley, M. Jennifer Kitil, Brian M. Galla, Susan Kaiser Greenland, Jill Locke, Eric Ishijima, and Connie Kasari. "Effects of Mindful Awareness Practices on Executive Functions in Elementary School Children." *Journal of Applied School Psychology* 26, no. 1 (2010): 70–95.

Galla, Brian M., David S. Black, and Susan Kaiser Greenland. "Mindfulness Training to Promote Self-Regulation in Youth: Effects of the Inner Kids Program." In *Handbook of Mindfulness in Education: Integrating Theory and Research into Practice*, edited by Kimberly A. Schonert-Reichl and Robert W. Roeser. New York: Springer, 2016.

Carle, Eric. *"Slowly, Slowly, Slowly," Said the Sloth.* New York: Philomel, 2002.

8. A Peaceful Heart

Goodman, Trudy. Personal interview, January 14, 2016.

Seppälä, Emma M. "18 Science-Backed Reasons to Try Loving-Kindness Meditation!" *Psychology Today*, September 15, 2014.

9. Out of Our Heads

Kabat-Zinn, Jon. *Coming to Our Senses: Healing Ourselves and the World through Mindfulness*. New York: Hyperion, 2005.

Willard, Christopher. *Growing Up Mindful: Essential Practices to Help Children, Teens, and Families Find Balance, Calm, and Resilience*. Boulder, CO: Sounds True, 2016.

Goodman, Trudy. Personal interview, January 14, 2016.

Part Four: Caring

Introduction

The story of an acrobat and his apprentice is based on "Sedaka Sutta: The Bamboo Acrobat." Translated by Andrew Olendzki. *Access to Insight*, 2005. Accessed January 18, 2016. www.accesstoinsight.org/tipitaka/sn/sn47/sn47.019.olen.html.

Thich Nhat Hanh. *Your True Home: The Everyday Wisdom of Thich Nhat Hanh*, edited by Melvin McLeod. Boston: Shambhala, 2011.

10. Is It Helpful?

His Holiness the Dalai Lama. *Beyond Religion: Ethics for a Whole World*. Boston: Houghton Mifflin Harcourt, 2011.

Bailey, Becky A. *Conscious Discipline: 7 Basic Skills for Brain Smart Classroom Management*. Oviedo, FL: Loving Guidance, 2001.

Chödrön, Pema. *Awakening Loving-Kindness*. Boston: Shambhala, 1996.

11. Floodlight of Attention

Mingyur, Yongey, Rinpoche, with Helen Tworkov. *Turning Confusion into Clarity: A Guide to the Foundation Practices of Tibetan Buddhism*. Boston: Shambhala, 2014.

Trungpa, Chögyam, Rinpoche. *Mindfulness in Action: Making Friends with Yourself through Meditation and Everyday Awareness*, edited by Carolyn Rose Gimian. Boston: Shambhala, 2015.

Greenberg, Mark. Personal interview, January 9, 2016.

Das, Surya, Lama. *Awakening to the Sacred: Creating a Spiritual Life from Scratch*. New York: Broadway, 1999.

————. Personal interview, March 27, 2012.

Part Five: Connecting

Introduction

Dubuc, Marianne. *The Lion and the Bird*. New York: Enchanted Lion, 2014.

The phrase "Let the music play" is a tip of the hat to Chögyam Trungpa Rinpoche's phrase "Let the phenomena play," which he introduced in his book *Crazy Wisdom*, edited by Sherab Chödzin. Boston: Shambhala, 1991.

12. To Be, Not to Seem

Bailey, Becky A. *Conscious Discipline: 7 Basic Skills for Brain Smart Classroom Management*. Oviedo, FL: Loving Guidance, 2001.

Winnicott, D. W. "Mirror-Role of the Mother and Family in Child Development." In *The Predicament of the Family: A Psycho-Analytical Symposium*, edited by P. Lomas, 26–33. London: Hogarth Press, 1967.

Epstein, Mark. *The Trauma of Everyday Life*. New York: Penguin, 2014.

Portis, Antoinette. *Not a Box*. New York: HarperCollins, 2006.

Banyai, Istvan. *Zoom*. New York: Viking, 1995.

13. Freedom

The story of the hummingbirds and an elephant is based on a Chinese folk story entitled "Holding Up the Sky."

Lyubomirsky, Sonja. *The How of Happiness: A Scientific Approach to Getting the Life You Want*. New York: Penguin, 2008.

McLeod, Ken. *Wake Up to Your Life: Discovering the Buddhist Path of Attention*. San Francisco: HarperSanFranciso, 2001.

His Holiness the Dalai Lama. *Beyond Religion: Ethics for a Whole World*. Boston: Houghton Mifflin Harcourt, 2011.

The story of a samurai and the tea master is based on a Japanese folk tale.

Seuss, Dr. *Oh, the Places You'll Go!* New York: Random House, 1990.

Ponlop, Dzogchen, Rinpoche. *Rebel Buddha: On the Road to Freedom.* Boston: Shambhala, 2010.

Wallace, David Foster. *This Is Water: Some Thoughts, Delivered on a Significant Occasion, about Living a Compassionate Life.* New York: Little, Brown, 2009.

ABOUT THE AUTHOR

Susan Kaiser Greenland is a mindfulness and meditation teacher. She has studied meditation with teachers from the Tibetan Buddhist tradition since 1997.

Susan worked as a corporate lawyer from 1988 to 2005. During that time she developed the Inner Kids program while volunteering in public schools teaching secular mindfulness. Inner Kids is a hybrid of classical mindfulness and meditation practices that have been adapted for children, and one of the first mindfulness programs in education. Susan and her husband, the author Seth Greenland, founded The Inner Kids Foundation, a not-for-profit organization that taught secular mindfulness in schools and community-based programs in the greater Los Angeles area from 2001 through 2009. She eventually left her law practice to work with children, teachers, and parents full-time.

Susan was on the clinical team of the Pediatric Pain Clinic at UCLA Mattel Children's Hospital, co-investigator on a UCLA research study on the impact of mindfulness in education, and a collaborator on an investigation of mindful eating for children and caregivers. Research on the Inner Kids elementary school program has been published in the *Journal of Applied School Psychology*.

Quoted in numerous magazines and newspapers, including the *New York Times*, the *Los Angeles Times*, the *Chicago Tribune*, the *Washington Post*, *USA Today*, *Real Simple*, and *Parents Magazine*, Susan has also written for the *Huffington Post* and other publications. She currently works in the United States and abroad as an author, public speaker, and educator on the subject of sharing secular mindfulness and meditation with children and families.

Susan and her husband live in Los Angeles, California, and have two grown children.